The Victor's Crown

David Potter is Arthur F. Thurnau Professor of Greek and Latin in the Department of Classical Studies at the University of Michigan. He is the author of *Emperors of Rome*, also from Quercus.

The Victor's Crown

How the Birth of the Olympics
and the Rise of the Roman Games
Changed Sport For Ever

David Potter

Quercus

First published in Great Britain in 2011 by Quercus

This edition published in 2012 by

Quercus
55 Baker Street
Seventh Floor, South Block
London
W1U 8EW

A CIP catalogue record for this book is available
from the British Library

ISBN 978 0 85738 200 9

10 9 8 7 6 5 4 3 2 1

Text and plates designed and typeset by Ellipsis

Printed and bound in Great Britain by Clays Ltd, St Ives plc

Contents

List of Illustrations   ix

Maps   xii

Preface   xv

Then and Now   xvii

PART 1: ASHES, LINEN AND THE ORIGINS OF SPORT

1: Introduction   3

2: Homer and the Bronze Age   13

3: Homer and Sport   24

PART 2: OLYMPIA

4: From Myth to History   37

5: Olympia in 480 BC   49

6: The Olympic Games of 476 BC   55

7: The Festival Approaches   62

8: Winning   67

   The equestrian events   67

   The pentathlon and the foot races   73

   Nudity   76

   Pain and suffering   78

9: Remembering Victory   89
  The athlete as hero   93
10: The Emergence of the Panhellenic Cycle   98

PART 3: THE WORLD OF THE GYMNASIUM

11: Sport and Civic Virtue   109
12: Beroia   127
13: Getting in Shape and Turning Pro   137

PART 4: ROMAN GAMES

14: Greece Meets Rome   163
15: Kings and Games   169
16: Rome and Italy   179
17: Actors and Gladiators   186
18: Caesar, Antony, Augustus and the Games   209

PART 5: IMPERIAL GAMES

19: Watching   225
20: The Fan's Experience   229
21: Expectations   233
22: Crowd Noise   237
23: Dreaming of Sport   242
24: Images of Sport   246
25: Women's Sports   252
26: Gladiators   258
  Life as a gladiator   259
  Training and ranking   262
  Dying   264
  Choosing to be a gladiator   269

CONTENTS

27: Charioteers   273
28: Athletes   278
    Athletic guilds   279
    Cheating   286
29: Running the Show   288
    Administration   292
    Athletics   300

Epilogue: The Long End of an Era   308
Bibliography   321
Classical Sources   350
Notes   359
Index   407

List of Illustrations

1. Evans' reconstruction of the Taureador fresco.
2. Marinatos' reconstruction of the Taureador fresco.
3. Terracotta image of a charioteer and horses from Olympia. © Olympia Archaeological Museum
4. Hoplitodromos. © Indiana University Museum
5. Panathenaic amphora with discus thrower and teacher by Euthymides, Museo Archeologico Nazionale, Naples, Italy. © Scala / Ministero Beni e Att. Culturali
6. Amphora with black figures engaged in a stadion race by Kleophrades, 500 - 490 BCE, Paris, Musée du Louvre. © Scala / White Images
7. Amphora depicting the end of a boxing match. © National Archaeological Museum, Athens
8. Two wrestlers. Hellenistic Bronze statuette from Alexandria, 2nd century BCE, Paris, Musée du Louvre. © akg-images / Erich Lessing
9. Wrestler about to drop his opponent on his head. Hellenistic Bronze statuette from Alexandria, 2nd century BCE, Paris, Musée du Louvre. © akg-images / Erich Lessing
10. Reconstruction of the Olympic site as it was in 476. © Matthew Harrington
11. The judge's box in the stadion at Olympia. © Matthew Harrington

12. Erotic scene depicting two male athletes engaged in homosexual intercourse. Terracotta black figure amphora, 5th century BCE, Museo Archeologico Nazionale, Naples, Italy. © Vanni / Art Resource, NY
13. Panathenaic prize amphora depicting a boxing contest, signed by the potter Kittos, made in Athens c. 367-366 BC. © The Trustees of the British Museum
14. Aerial view of the site of Olympia. © CORBIS / Yann Arthus-Bertrand
15. Paestum tomb painting of Gladiatorial combat. Lucanian funerary fresco, 4th–3rd century BCE. © Alinari / Topfoto
16. Paestum tomb painting of a chariot race and gladiatorial combat. Lucanian funerary fresco. 4th–3rd-century BCE © Alinari / Topfoto
17. The costly *munus* (public show and gift) offered by Magerius. Roman mosaic from Smirat (near Moknine). Mid 3rd-century CE. © CORBIS / Ruggero Vanni
18. Reconstruction of the amphitheatre. © Matthew Harrington
19. Restoration of the early 3rd-century CE gladiator mosaic at the Wadi Ledbda by Mohammed Ali Drogui. Leptis Magna, Libya. © akg-images / Gilles Mermet
20. Dar Buc Ammera Mosaic © Sebastia Giralt
21. Marble relief with female gladiators, Roman, 1st-2nd century AD. From Halikarnassos (modern Bodrum, Turkey). © The Trustees of the British Museum
22. Tombstone of Paralos and wife, Hierapolis.
23. The execution scene from Hierapolis

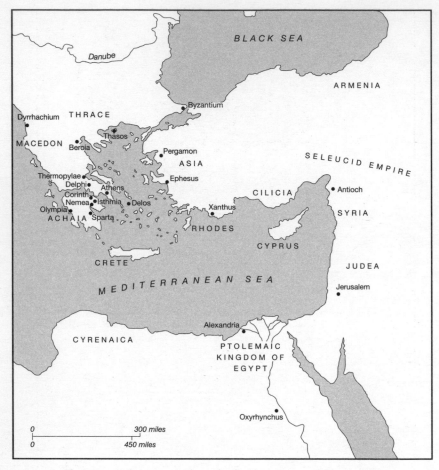

The Eastern Mediterranean (with significant athletic sites mentioned in the text)

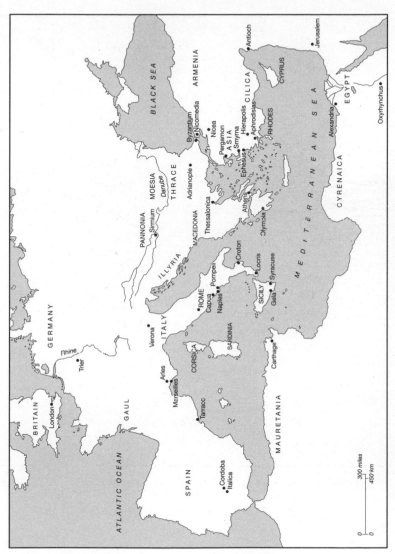

The Roman Empire

Preface

This book began some twenty years ago when my friend Ludwig Koenen, then chair of my department, asked me to take over a long-standing course on ancient sport. The many students who have taken the course over the years have continued to spark my interest in the subject, and I want here to register my profound appreciation both of them and of the generations of graduate students who have borne much of the teaching workload with me and helped the course to evolve. I am very grateful to Richard Milbank at Quercus who took this project on, to Richard Milner who has seen it into press, Josh Ireland who has overseen production and for the exceptional talent of Sue Phillpott who copy edited the book.

In the last five years it has been my great good fortune to serve as a member of the University of Michigan's Advisory Board on Intercollegiate Athletics, and, as chairman of the governing committee of the faculty senate for one of those years, to look at the business of sport with a fresh eye. I am profoundly grateful to President Mary Sue Coleman and Bill Martin, the athletic director while this book was being written, for their support in these tasks. I have also had the opportunity to meet and work with some truly remarkable coaches and athletic administrators, including Lloyd Carr, Carol

Hutchins, Ronni Bernstein (who also revived my tennis game), Judy Van Horn, Mike Stevenson, Greg Harden and Bitsy Ritt, as well as my colleagues on the board, Bruno Giordani and Stan Berent.

In writing this book I have received exemplary assistance from Nellie Kippley (a veteran of Roman sport and former captain of the Michigan Women's Gymnastics Team) who helped me understand modern training techniques and the experience of athletes at the highest level of intercollegiate competition. I have also received invaluable assistance from Matt Newman, a student in the UM's Graduate Program in Classical Philology. Others who offered sage advice on earlier versions include Mike Sampson, Karen Acton and Nate Andrade. I am also enormously grateful to a number of colleagues, especially Arthur Verhoogt, who read most of the manuscript, Sara Forsdyke, who guided me through the history of Greece, and Chris Ratté, a sure guide on archaeological issues. My most important source of support and comfort has been, as ever, my family – Ellen, Claire and Natalie.

Then and Now

It is the night of 9 July 2006. In Berlin, Fabio Grosso's penalty kick eludes French goalkeeper Fabien Barthez. The huge crowd in Rome's Circo Massimo erupts. Italy has won its fourth World Cup in front of 260 million spectators, drawn all around the world to television sets or giant screens such as those in the Circo. Never had so many human beings watched a single event. But it is with those gathered in the Circo Massimo that we will begin. They link our world with another which, though long gone, may still, in many ways, help us understand our own.

Buildings hold not only people, they also hold stories, and it is by looking at some of these stories that we may begin to see how these two worlds – the world of the iPod and the cell-phone on the one hand, that of the stylus and papyrus roll on the other – have so much in common. The Circo Massimo is a case in point. It is the site of the ancient Circus Maximus where, for well over a thousand years, hundreds of thousands of Romans sat each year to watch chariots tear seven times around the six-hundred-metre track in a race that would ultimately cover four miles – far longer than the most challenging events in US and English thoroughbred racing – and be punctuated by crashes and breakdowns as well as by feats of astonishing skill.

Every race that was ever run in the Circus Maximus generated a tale of its own, but the story of the Circus Maximus is also an integral part of the story of Rome, of the city's growth as it came to rule a powerful empire. The Circus Maximus was a symbol of the forces that drew its people together. At one time it had simply been a track in the valley between the Palatine and Aventine Hills. The Palatine was the centre of royal and aristocratic power, over-looking the Roman Forum on one side, the centre of political life. The Aventine, supporting a temple in honour of the goddess of grain, would become the focal point of movements that looked to restrain the power of the aristocracy. The symbolic importance of the great sporting ground that lay between these two points, offering an alternative to the Forum as a place for people to come together, was not lost upon the Romans themselves. Not surprisingly, then, some of the aristocracy wished to make their mark on the space, to show how their own achievements might not only glorify their families (a major interest of Roman nobles) but also benefit the community of Romans as a whole. So it was that by the beginning of the fifth century BC, members of Rome's aristocracy decided that their deeds would be better remembered if they could have perman-ent seats along the race track. These were the first permanent structures in the area, and their existence is testimony to an eternal theme in the history of sport as entertainment: that the spectators are as much a part of the performance as it is possible for them to be, and that people will be drawn together by sport in ways they might otherwise not be. Jack Nicholson and David Beckham are hardly the first celebrities to take their seats at sporting events where they can be seen as well as see, but, whether they would care to admit it or not, they are aspects of a sociological phenomenon that helps explain why the games they love to watch are there for all of us.

With the passing of time, and as the sport of chariot-racing gained clout, the circus ground gradually began to fill up with more permanent buildings – most importantly a full-blown starting gate with elaborate mechanisms in place to ensure a fair start for everyone.[1] For the average fan, however, there was no seating except on temporary wooden stands. One reason for this was practical – the track had to be able to drain, and you couldn't have permanent seats unless you built a drain first. The other was ideological. Permanent buildings of stone for entertainment purposes were for Greeks, and Greeks were self-indulgent, unlike the Romans whose chief attribute would always be their *virtus*, or 'manliness'. So the Romans thought – but any prejudice can give way to power, and the meaning of something can be understood anew.

So it was in the case of the great stone buildings at Rome, and when the spectacularly successful general, Pompey, inserted himself for ever into the urban landscape by attaching a gigantic theatre to a temple, a stone circus became a possibility.[2] It was Julius Caesar, Pompey's rival and ultimate conqueror, who dug the necessary drainage ditch and started building marble seats to surround the track. When Caesar chose to ignore the perils that threatened him on the Ides of March, the grand plans were left unrealized, only to be brought to fruition after years of civil war by his heir, the emperor Augustus, who transformed the building in part into a victory monument. There would be new lap-counters, in the form of dolphins (whose noses, pointing up at the beginning of the race, would be depressed one by one as the laps flew by). There was also the Egyptian obelisk, to remind everyone that the last battle in the great war had been against the Queen of Egypt – the famous Cleopatra – and her besotted lover, the Roman Mark Antony.

It would be more than a century before more work was done on the Circus Maximus, and this time the agent would be Trajan, a man whose claim to the throne depended upon his adoption by an old man who was under siege from his own imperial guard. Trajan, the son of a famous general, happened at that time to be in command of a large army, and his improvements (he completed the marblification of the circus seats) were a way of symbolizing his attachment to the people of Rome. In so doing he was following the example not only of Augustus, but also of his father's old boss, the emperor Vespasian (winner of another civil war) who tore down part of a predecessor's massive house to erect the almost equally massive amphitheatre now known as the Colosseum. That too was a victory monument, for some part of the cost was paid from treasure taken from the Jewish temple at Jerusalem which his son Titus destroyed in AD 70.[3]

'While stands the Coliseum, Rome shall stand; when falls the Coliseum, Rome shall fall; and when Rome falls – the World':[4] thus Lord Byron rendered a saying of English pilgrims that appeared in a work attributed to Bede, the esteemed eighth-century man of letters. In 1954, when cracks appeared in the façade of the building, there were many who thought that the end was nigh.[5] We're still here, and so is the Colosseum, but we still attach meaning to big buildings where sports are played. They mean more to us than just victory and defeat, or the thrill of competition. They can be statements about who we are, about where we are going or where we have been. The massive construction projects for the Athens Olympics in 2004, and the spectacular structures assembled in Beijing, symbolize national arrival on the world scene; magnificent opening ceremonies are statements of culture and pride while at the same time offering athletes the chance to shine.[6]

In New York City, at the end of the 2008 baseball season, two stadia were closed for good, to be replaced by modern structures the following season. The closure of Yankee Stadium was marked with spectacular ceremony, while fans of the Mets complained that their own ground received no such glorious send-off.[7] But then, Shea Stadium was not 'the house that Ruth built', where Joe Louis struck a blow for civilization against the Aryan ideology of Adolf Hitler by knocking out Max Schmeling, or where the game that placed the National Football League on the map was played. In a very real way the old Yankee Stadium represented more than the Yankees: it represented the burgeoning of professional sport in America. The decision to tear it down and replace it with a new stadium was immensely controversial, not just because of the huge cost – imposed in part upon the taxpayers of New York – but also because of the site's history. Nor was it lost on some Yankee fans that while their stadium awaited the wrecking ball, the rival Boston Red Sox decided to preserve their ageing home in Fenway Park by simply modifying it (while also raising ticket prices).

Such stories raise a core question about the role of sport in society as a whole: quite simply, why should anyone bother to be involved in something that can be a costly hassle and in which about half those concerned are guaranteed to be losers about half of the time? The overarching question is this: why, in this day and age, do sports matter so much to so many people? There have been only two periods in human history when this has been so. Aside from our own time, the other encompasses the centuries of Roman dominance in the Mediterranean world – the first century BC to the seventh AD – and, in the regions of Greece and Italy particularly, from the seventh century BC onwards.

There is a direct and rather peculiar link between the ancient world of sport and the modern, a link provided by three men: Evangelos Zappas, Dr William Penny Brookes and Baron Pierre de Coubertin. Inspired by calls to refound the ancient Olympics by the poet and newspaperman Panagiotis Soutsos, Zappas sponsored

the first 'modern' Olympics at Athens in 1856. It was an astonishing thing to do. The sports of the ancient Olympic games – foot
races, boxing, wrestling, chariot-racing and so forth – were no longer
features of organized athletics. In fact, other than the games played
in schools (mostly English), the only one that had an international
aspect in these years was cricket. Played in England since the Middle
Ages (people were arrested for playing it rather than attending
church in 1661), cricket had been exported to the English colonies,
where it was domesticated to such an extent that the first international cricket match was actually played between the United States
and Canada in 1841.[8] Outside of Greece, the only person who seems
to have been interested in the sort of sports that interested Soutsos
and Zappas was Dr Brookes, born in Much Wenlock in Shropshire
in 1809. He had founded the Wenlock Olympian Class, which combined some ancient games with cricket and the nascent game of
football, thrown in for good measure, to 'promote the moral, physical and intellectual improvement of the inhabitants of the Town
and neighbourhood of Wenlock'.[9] Brookes, who seems to have been
a genuinely decent human being, was intrigued by the Greek project
and sent £10 to fund a prize when the first games were held in
1859; and he adopted games from Athens for the games he organized at Wenlock.

The approach that Zappas and Brookes took to sport was intensely
controversial, in that they believed that anyone should be allowed
to play, regardless of social class. Outrage at Brookes's egalitarian
athletic event in 1859 led in England to the foundation of the
Amateur Athletic Club in 1866, which was designed to restrict participation in sports to 'amateurs and gentlemen'.[10] This was in effect
just as much a revival (though the founders of the AAC did not
know it at the time) of Greek habits as were the Olympic Games
themselves: participation was limited in the classical world to the

ancient equivalent of 'gentlemen', though those gentlemen expected to be handsomely rewarded and there was no concept of 'amateur' in the British sense. Undaunted, Brookes continued to spread his gospel of universal participation in sports at home, triumphing with a spectacular set of National Olympic Games at the Crystal Palace in 1866, the year after Zappas died.

In 1870 a new Olympic committee at Athens revived Zappas's games in the new Panathenaic stadium, built on the site of the ancient stadium of Herodes Atticus, which had been excavated with more of Zappas's money – then promptly killed them in 1875, when the committee declared that only gentlemen would be eligible to compete.[11] In 1888, meeting in the newly constructed Zappcion in Athens's National Garden (again, financed posthumously by Zappas and housing his head), the Olympic committee decided to try again. After a series of missteps, a new figure intervened in Pierre de Coubertin. Since the French defeat at the hands of Germany in 1870, de Coubertin had been interested in athletics as a way of reinvigorating France by making its educational system 'more English'. His inspirations included *Tom Brown's School Days* and Brookes's Olympics, but his contacts were very different from those of the earlier pioneers, including as they did an American academic who was chairman of the Ivy Collegiate Faculty Committee, the founder of the Stockholm Gymnastics Association, an English aristocrat, the secretary of Britain's Amateur Athletic Association as well as a German, a Czech and a Russian. De Coubertin's partners' experience thus tended to link education with athletics, and that also meant a tendency to want participation limited to 'gentlemen'.[12] It was this that led the Olympic committee to insist that participants be 'amateurs', and even to insist – on the basis of deeply flawed research – that this had been the case in the ancient world they were seeking to resuscitate.

Moving with a combination of immense energy and wealth – a crucial component in all these efforts – de Coubertin created a new International Olympic Committee in Paris, based on his own connections, all of whom were strongly committed to the ideal of gentlemanly amateur sport. Summoning the first meeting of the International Olympic Committee, he managed to take from Zappas the credit for the enterprise, convince the Crown Prince of Greece to sponsor the games and organize the first truly International Olympic Games at Athens in 1896.[13]

From the start de Coubertin did what Brookes would not do: he created terms of engagement that reflected what he and his contemporaries imagined to be the ancient Greek ideal of amateurism. This was perhaps inevitable at the height of America's 'Gilded Age', when notions of equality were equated with socialism and team sports like football (in the European sense of the word) were seen as games for working men, and thus not the sort of thing that should be sanctioned by an official body of gentlemen who were interested in creating prizes for people who, they felt, shared their values. It is perhaps not coincidental that the Amateur Athletic Club was formed three years after the formation of England's Football Association in 1863. Would Brookes's somewhat eccentric effort to promote games for the working man have aroused such annoyance if the rise of the working man's game had not been in the offing as well?

Successful as de Coubertin was, he could not control the forces unleashed by the Olympic movement. It was the very internationalism of the Olympics that set them apart from the school sports that were rapidly attracting a national following (American football in the United States and Rugby in the rest of the English-speaking world) and from 'working-class' sports that were developing their own professional leagues (football in Europe, baseball in the United States). It was that same internationalism that made Olympic sports fair game for the advocates of the most deadly of all the forces unleashed by the twentieth century: nationalism. From 1956 to 1986, the Olympics became a surrogate venue for the Cold War as both the Soviet bloc and the nations of NATO sought to validate their social systems through success on the playing field. But why should that be? Why should sporting events have become surrogates for international politics? Why should a man of no athletic talent whatsoever – Adolf Hitler – have tried to make his Berlin Olympic games a showcase for the superiority of the Aryan race? These questions bring us back again to what our world of sport has in common with that of the Greeks and Romans.

The answer to that question may, at first glance, seem immensely simple. It resides in the very word 'athlete' or, in Greek, *athlêtês*. The word literally means a person who competes for a prize. Unlike other forms of physical activity that could serve as entertainment, it was the competition, the uncertainty about who would be the very best on any given day, that set competitive sport apart from any other activity.[14] In the ideal world, the prize had to be won through the expenditure of the contestant's sweat, effort, skill and, at times, blood. The outcome must be uncertain (or at least formally uncertain) at the outset. Beforehand, spectators form their own opinion as to which contestant should win, and they can join in the contest – in many places – by putting a bet on the event. For some it may be the only opinion truly their own that they express openly. Honour goes to the victor only with the agreement of the spectators that he or she has truly deserved to win. Sports develop as part of a constant dialogue between whoever takes charge of an event and the people who come to watch. If the games are boring or if the team is bad, the fans can simply stay away.

The freedom to stay away is another free choice, and an

important one. In the ancient world where competitive sports began, true freedom was a very rare commodity. It is precisely in the one region of the ancient world where royal power was absent that an independent sporting culture was born. Athletics developed in Greece rather than in Egypt, even though there was a tradition of violent sport for the entertainment of the pharaoh, or in Mesopotamia, even though there too we have records of physical contests provided for the amusement of rulers. Once competitive sports do develop, tyrants, dictators and kings may try to harness them to their own purpose, as Hitler did with the Berlin Olympics. But even then, the great power has to concede ground to the athlete, and even to the fan. Hitler could refuse to attend a medal ceremony for the great African-American track star Jesse Owens, but he could not take the medal away. Indeed the characteristics that link modern sport with that of the ancient world are the theoretical equality as between performers, along with specialization (there are some cross-over athletes in the ancient world, as in the modern, but they are invariably exceptional figures), bureaucratization, elaborate systems of rules and a passion for the history of sport.[15]

The dialogue of sport has always been ignited by the divergent interests of three groups: those with the money to sponsor events (let's call them the owners, for now) who are implicitly in competition with their peers (a crucial factor that limits their ability to 'fix' the outcome of an event), the athletes and the fans. Given that they are competing against others of their ilk, owners have an interest in sponsoring events that make them look good, and to that end they will occasionally give way to the interests of the athletes (largely by paying them more), and at times also to the fans, usually by trying to get the athletes to do something new, different and possibly dangerous. This enables the fans to feel that they have some control. It also creates very strong feelings about who athletes should be and how they should act. Athletes never just represent themselves, no matter how much they would like to, or feel that they really do, as the golfer Tiger Woods learned when details of his extracurricular activities became public knowledge. They always represent their fans too, and must embody some qualities that the fans feel are important. Usually these will be integrity, toughness and skill. Sometimes it will also include the bloody-minded courage to face a seemingly impossible task.

The crucial feature of sport is, then, not simply the contest, but the way it enables those outside the arena to feel linked with those within, and in so doing to feel (at least briefly) empowered by what they do. It is this aspect of sport that energizes and creates communities. It allows people to find themselves insiders in the game. And it is precisely these aspects that so infuriate many who think that the whole exercise is a massive waste of time and money, and who feel excluded from it, for whatever reason. For while sport may build community it can also alienate, or provide venues within which the otherwise alienated may gather. Roman chariot-racing and pantomime dancing gave rise to chariot and pantomime riots amongst diehard supporters, in the same way that football matches enable hooliganism. Hooligans sometimes mingle extremist political views with their extremist fandom, or, in the North American version of the sport, with routine post-game riots around some college campuses, such as the one in Columbus, Ohio.

Fans talk, cheer, argue and riot; they can also influence what it is that they see. One of the driving forces behind the development of different sports in the ancient world was plainly fan interest. Indeed, as we move forward into that world we see sports of roughly three kinds: those in which the athlete performs on his own (we will be concerned with women as athletes only when we get into the period of Roman domination, towards the end of the first century BC); those that involve athletes using some sort of tool (be it chariot or weapon); and those in which the athlete either combines basic sports of the non-tool-using variety, or uses the tools in an unusual way.

Sports of the third category tend to be driven by the interests of fans and might take the form of 'races of champions', which we find in the context of chariot races in the Circus Maximus; or races in which charioteers are forced to race with teams of horses that are not their own (very dangerous) or with teams of more than four horses (even more dangerous).[16] For instance, gladiators who in the Roman world typically fought with dull weapons might find that a games sponsor had caved in to popular pressure to obtain special permission from the imperial government to have them fight with sharp ones.[17] At least this was better than the very rare occasions when a gladiator would find himself involved in a fight where death was the anticipated outcome (this required a special imperial dispensation), and which he might only agree to if the sponsor undertook to guarantee his funeral expenses! Perhaps most obvious of all in this respect, though, is the Greek sport of pancration, or all-in fighting, which combined elements of boxing and wrestling and tended to recruit participants from those two sports. One writer suggests that the original training of a pancratiast as a boxer or wrestler would continue to show throughout his career.[18] Other sorts of fan-driven activity might have been races in armour (no athlete in his right mind would design a race that required him to carry a shield as he ran), or the rather odd (to us) event known as 'chariot-hopping' in which the contestants jumped in and out of the chariot as it moved.[19]

Before there was a chariot-hopper or a runner in armour, or even a wrestler, there had to be a prize, a tangible reward for which the athlete could contend and that could be awarded only for actual merit. This is not pay for a performance – it is something for which the athlete puts himself at risk with no guarantee of success or reward; success, and even, at times, failure, will give him some claim to a place in the minds of the fans. And both the athlete and the fan will be aware that competition is not limited just to the day of the event, but to the history of previous performances – ancient athletes were every bit as obsessive about their records as their modern counterparts, and this is reflected in the passion of fans.

In general terms, the usual trajectory that sport (ancient or modern) follows is towards making events more dangerous and/or more expensive. When the increased danger or cost clashes with other social values, society's interest in regulation, in limiting the danger of the competition or in restraining cost, tends to give way to the demand for better and more interesting entertainment until some sort of scandal – to do for instance, with cheating, excessive violence, or bankruptcy – strengthens the hand of would-be regulators. At that point some regulation will be possible, but it will not ordinarily have a long-term effect – one of the earliest texts that survives from ancient Olympia prohibits finger-breaking in wrestling (which happened anyway), while efforts to limit the costs and the lethality of gladiatorial combat succeeded or failed depending upon the amount of effort Roman imperial authorities were willing to put into regulation. It is only when fans lose interest, or management can no longer afford to support sport, that actual change will occur.

To understand the history of ancient sport we must examine how these events for prizes came into being, as well as how athletes and fans changed the original events to suit themselves. The development of ancient sport cannot be traced to a specific time, but rather, as with sport in the modern world, it has to be seen in the context of changes in society as a whole, as part of a process of development that does not follow a single course. The creation of regular festivals in Greece for the awarding of prizes to athletes will not explain everything; it will not explain athletes' pay scales, the creation of professional associations, or riots. The creation of the first sporting festival, is, however, a significant point in triggering the processes that brought people together at games and that made the games important parts of their lives. And so it is to the beginning of those processes that we shall now turn.

PART 1

Ashes, Linen and the Origins of Sport

1

Introduction[1]

It is late afternoon and the funeral pyre has burned itself out. Members of the family gather the bones of the dead man, wrap them in yellow cloth, and place them in a copper urn with some dried pomegranates as an offering to the gods of the Underworld. The ceremony is as he had wished it, for it was done as the poets sang about such things. The funeral games would have been magnificent, for that too was what the poets sang.

The copper urn killed the microbes that would ordinarily have destroyed the shroud, preserving it (and the memory of the ceremony) for thousands of years until Greek archaeologists uncovered it.[2] In doing so they may have recovered not only some of the earliest fabric known from Western Europe, but also some of our earliest evidence – albeit indirect – for the history of sport. With the aid of this, and other fabrics that have been preserved in the same way from roughly the same period – from the beginning of the eleventh to the end of the eighth centuries BC, once known as the Dark Age of Greek history – we can begin to understand how the foundations of Greek entertainment and sporting culture were laid. As a result of new discoveries we can see light in areas where all once seemed dark, and find patterns in evidence that was once so sparse that no rhyme or reason could emerge. We can begin to trace the history of human imagination in Greece, and as we do so, we can recreate the world in which what we recognize as our traditions of sport began to take shape.

Fabrics found in other funerary urns are survivors of immensely elaborate funerals, involving the incineration of the deceased upon a massive pyre. Much effort was expended in creating such a pyre, for there were no supplies of dried wood lying about in the Greek cities of the era, awaiting disposal with the dead. The wood had to be freshly cut, as we are told in one of the great set-pieces in Homer's *Iliad* – amongst the oldest surviving and greatest works of Greek literature. Here, in order to send Patroclus (the beloved of the hero Achilles) to the Underworld, Agamemnon, the most powerful of the Greeks at Troy, ordered men to cut the wood for the pyre on a nearby mountain. Agamemnon's instruction was one stage in the process of reconciliation that occupies Homer in the last two books of his great epic, which had begun as a tale of wrath. It was a quarrel over precedence between Achilles and Agamemnon that set the tragedy of the *Iliad* in action, and it is not until the end of the twenty-third book that the two men are fully reconciled. In the meantime Achilles had destroyed the man he loved most, allowing Patroclus to take his own place in the fighting, so that he fell victim to his pride, the gods and the weapons of Hector, the most distinguished of the Trojans. Achilles had slain Hector (and countless other Trojans) in revenge, but now he lived not with his beloved, but rather with the corpses of Patroclus and Hector – the one from which he could not bear to be parted, the other which the gods themselves had prevented him from dishonouring as he wished.

It had taken an apparition of Patroclus' spirit, begging that his body be properly buried, to convince Achilles that it was time to say farewell. He would do so in the grandest of styles, and so it was that on the night before the pyre would be built, Achilles had treated his personal followers to a great banquet as they lamented Patroclus. On the day of the funeral, these same followers bore the corpse to the new pyre, covering it with locks of their hair. When they put the body down, Achilles coated it in the fat of dead animals so that it would burn all the faster. He then slaughtered offerings at other points around the pyre – the two dogs and four horses have parallels in the archaeological record, the twelve 'shining sons of the Trojans' who joined them do not – before leaving a lock of his own hair.

The damp oak would not burn until a pair of somewhat inebriated gods of the winds showed up to huff and puff until the flames exploded. It would take all night for the fire to subside, and in the morning the embers had to be cooled with offerings of wine so that the ashes of Patroclus could be recovered and placed, coated with a double layer of animal fat, in a bronze bowl covered with linen, there to await the time, now inevitable and close, at which the ashes of Achilles himself would join them. The fire had been extinguished by the assembled Greeks, not just by the primary mourners, and it was the army that cast down the sides of the retaining wall around the pyre to form a tumulus, low at first, to be made much larger when Achilles' own ashes would be mixed with those of Patroclus.

There is an enormous tumulus overlooking the Dardanelles near the site of Troy that later travellers assumed was that of the heroes. There are (or were) others, at Lefkandi on Euboea in Greece, and on Cyprus in a city settled by Greeks, that help link the vision of Homer with the real world. At Lefkandi excavators discovered a burial mound covering a building that was once 150 feet long. In the midst of it are two burials, one of a once-powerful woman. Her body was not burned but laid to rest with sumptuous gifts. The other is an urn, covered in linen, that holds the ashes of a man who was perhaps once the master of the house. Nearby are the bones of four horses and weapons of war, surely those once borne by that man. For other, later generations the great tomb was a focal point, as it is surrounded by more than a hundred burials, eighty of them graves, and another thirty-two the remains of pyres. On Cyprus, from later centuries, there are other burials, many with horses, some with urns that once held other offerings; and in one, the amphorae that held the wine that was used to douse the flames. In another tomb there is the skeleton of a man, bound, who accompanied the deceased on what became their final journey.[3]

It was only after the ashes had been gathered and the first tumulus erected that Achilles summoned the whole Greek army, and brought out the prizes to be won in the games honouring Patroclus. It is here that we join the history of sport in the Western world, though it must be admitted that the experience of doing so is like tuning into a game at half-time. We need to go back well before Homer was singing in the late eighth century BC and look at how the tradition that he knew came into being.

Homer was an oral poet. This seemingly simple statement is fraught with consequences and questions. Not the least of these is how is it, if Homer sang and was illiterate, that we have these poems, and what relationship does the world he describes bear to any historical society? In all probability, Homer recited his poems to a scribe in a form that was not too different from – though certainly not identical to – the works that we now read. Other people later added individual lines, and in some cases (we think) whole episodes, but the basic stories of the wrath of Achilles in the tenth year of the siege of Troy that comprises our *Iliad*, and the return of Odysseus to his wife and family on the island of Ithaca that makes up our *Odyssey*, were probably the work of one man.

Homer himself, however, was not the only person to have sung of the war at Troy – we have descriptions of many other poems on the subject by poets who were singing at about the same time – and he depended on a tradition that stretched back many centuries. In composing his work, Homer relied heavily upon formulae (set expressions that could fill out part of a line) and some very long set-pieces such as descriptions of the ways warriors put on their armour, or lists of peoples who joined the fighting. Thus, while Homer did not memorize a poem per se, he carried all the building blocks in his head. Readers of a translation like Richmond Lattimore's splendid version of the *Iliad* will feel these building blocks in phrases like the 'wine-dark sea' (*oinops pontos*), 'rosy-fingered dawn' (*rhododacktylos Eos*),' swift-footed Achilles' (*hôkus podas Achilleus*) and 'steep Ilium' (*Ilios aipeinê*).

Ilium is an alternative name for Troy, and this phrase brings us a further level of complexity, as it appears to have been modelled on a phrase in the Luwian language of what is now western Turkey. It seems to translate the formula that figures in several texts – *awienta Wilusa*, 'from steep Ilium'. Elsewhere (such as the description of a helmet made out of the tusks of wild boars) Homer is describing what was standard equipment centuries before his time, but not when he was alive. His version of the descent of Aphrodite seems to belong to a very ancient stratum of mythology reflecting contacts with the east that may be contemporary with the point at which a Luwian formula could have entered an earlier form of the Greek language, many hundreds of years in the past. Likewise the most powerful Greek king, Agamemnon, ruled a kingdom, Mycenae, that had not existed for centuries, and Troy itself had long since ceased to be a place of significance.

The world that Homer's story and his language look back to was one when Greece was divided into a number of kingdoms, ruled from palaces by kings who were called *wanaktes* (singular: *wanax*), and when records were kept in an early form of the Greek language. The archaeologists who uncovered these palaces also found clay tablets written in this early form of Greek, hardened by the fires that destroyed the palaces. It is to one of these tablets that we owe one of the most striking discoveries of recent years. The tablet in question comes from Thebes, and on it we find three cities mentioned in the order that they appear in the list of Greek forces that Homer provides in the second book of the *Iliad*. Two of these cities no longer existed in his time, so this discovery virtually proves that Homer must have been using a list of cities that had been passed down in the tradition for hundreds of years. We call the people who lived in these cities, and their age, 'Mycenaean', from the city of Agamemnon. To judge from those who were their contemporaries in Egypt and Turkey, they called themselves Achaeans and Danaans, both terms also known to Homer.[4]

Homer did not remember history, but there are shadowy suggestions in his verse that he remembered in very general terms a process by which the society ruled by kings in palaces, that of the Danaans and Achaeans, changed profoundly. He knew stories about a destructive war between the two great kingdoms in Greece, and his tradition knew the geography of Troy with surprising accuracy – and that Troy had once been a great city, which it was decidedly not in Homer's own time. His tradition sensed that the wars around Troy in the east had unpleasant consequences for many – a great number of heroes died, others found bitter welcomes when they came home. There is perhaps here a sense that it was the succession of wars that caused the collapse of the system run by the great kings and of the great fortified palaces in which they lived – at Mycenae itself, and at Tiryns in the plain of Argos a few miles distant, at Thebes in Boeotia as well as the nearby sites of Orchomenos and Gla. The impression of a society where violence and status were heavily intertwined that emerges from this tradition may also be correlated with observable naming patterns for Bronze Age people in Greece – most striking here is the high percentage of names that commemorate military activity and the god of war (Ares). Thus, the word for 'fighting force' being *lâwos*, we find characters such as Ekhelâwôn ('he who is victorious in [or over] the army'), Lâwoqwhontas ('he who kills the army'), Wisulos ('he who plunders') and Ahorimenês ('he who resists with his sword').[5]

The fires that had destroyed the great fortified palaces, as well as the unfortified palace at Pylos, had all blazed within the few years between 1200 and 1150 BC, some four centuries before Homer sang. The tradition that he knew might intimate this world, and possibly help explain what happened, but no more than that. Homer had never heard of a Hittite empire centred at Hattusa (Bogazkoy, in the heart of modern Turkey), nor did he know of the great king Hatusilis III, who complained bitterly to the king of the people he called the Ahhijawa (Homer's Achaeans, surely) about the actions of the adventurer Pijamiradu around Miletus in what is now western Turkey. The tradition may not even have recorded the name of Ekhelâwôn, who seems to have been the last *wanax* at Pylos. Yet it is with this tradition that all that we know of as classical Greek history must start, as well as the remains that have come to light through the labours of generations of increasingly sophisticated archaeologists; it is thanks to them, and to the immensely able linguists who have laboured on the clay tablets in the years after the brilliant decipherment of those texts as an early form of Greek by Michael Ventris in 1952.[6] It is from these texts that we get some vague sense of the position of the ruler in the palace – the *wanax* – and his assistants. These included one who would hold the title of *lawagetas*, or 'people gatherer', who was assisted by 'collectors'

9

and, at Pylos at least, by 'followers'. These were all officials attached to a central palace bureaucracy, and from Pylos again we hear of provincial governors who were appointed by the *wanax*. It is only outside these exalted circles that we find other people who seem to have been locally based, or in charge of specific trade groups – the title of one, in charge of the bronze smiths at Pylos, was *qu-si-re-u*.

There seems, within a few generations, to have grown up a sense that the old rulers represented something greater than the world succeeding them, which could not now recreate their grandeur. In the century after the destruction of the palaces some rudimentary efforts were made to reoccupy some of the sites, and a significant reoccupation of at least one of them took place. But the palaces were not rebuilt in anything like their former glory, and even the resettlements were attenuated. By about 1070 these efforts had come to an end, but now people began to look back in new ways on the rulers of the past. By 1100 BC, offerings had started to be left in tombs connected with the old regimes, and it was not uncommon by the time the master of the house was laid to rest at Lefkandi (c. 950) for people in other parts of Greece to leave offerings at old tombs of the time of the *wanaktes* as if they had been superior beings. None of these men, or women, had ever been burned in a great pyre, however; this was a habit that began to spread only after the destruction of the palaces. The palace rulers were laid to rest with offerings appropriate to their status, in grand tombs that were still visible in a countryside where no one could now command the labour needed to build such a thing. The development of 'tomb cults' is perhaps not unrelated to the continued interest in songs about the 'old days' as a way of defining status in the present, but it is also a reminder that the customs of the old days were not passed on intact.[7] The world was always changing, and it is with this in mind that we must interrogate the tradition, to see if it can tell us anything about the origin of the games that Homer describes, and anything about the way sport, as we would recognize it, came into being.

Book 23 of the *Iliad* not only gives us our grandest description of a funeral, it also gives us our most extensive description of funeral games. The eighth book of the *Odyssey* gives us an account of rather different games, held by King Alcinous of the Phaeacians (a mythical people who later Greeks decided lived on the island of Corfu). Given that different games are described in Homer's two works, and that at one point in the twenty-third book the elderly hero Nestor describes funeral games that are quite different from those of Achilles, how can we know what constituted Greek sport in this era, and whether these traditions go back centuries before Homer's time or were emerging even as he sang? Was the athletic tradition in Homer's verse the product of the age of courts and kings, or was it the product of a new age when the courts and kings had vanished and men strove for status on an equal footing?

There is certainly evidence for physical contests and entertainments, both in the Greek world and in the lands of their powerful Near Eastern neighbours, that resemble or anticipate contests that Homer describes. The problem is that we can almost never know the status of the contestants, and rarely find a clear statement as to the nature of the event in which they displayed their talents. What is clear, though, is that the style of funeral that Patroclus was given in the *Iliad*, and those that we can see in the archaeological record, does not go back to the era of the palaces in Greece. The bodies of the great and famous in that age were not cremated. On the other hand, the burial at Lefkandi suggests that the general switch to spectacular cremation did not occur very long after the palaces were destroyed, and evidence from another site (Tanagra in nearby Boeotia in central Greece) suggests that, amongst people who did not live in palaces, the transition began before the end of the palatial period. The variation in practices that has been uncovered on Cyprus and elsewhere reminds us that there were no handbooks telling people how to dispose of their dead – rather, there was a smorgasbord of practices that emerged over time, and a funeral would be assembled from events that people had seen or heard of on other occasions or in other places. When we look at the games in Homer we might be better advised to ask not when specific events came into being or were excluded, but rather when it seems likely that the menu of our athletic feast began to be composed and developed.[8]

2

Homer and the Bronze Age

The games in Book 23 of the *Iliad* consist of eight events: a chariot race, a foot race, boxing, wrestling, the throwing of large stones, duels between spearmen to first blood, archery and spear-throwing (using, it seems, the regular hand-to-hand weapons of warriors whose primary weapon was the heavy spear rather than a javelin). In the midst of these games, the old hero Nestor describes some in which he starred – games held 'when the Epeians buried powerful Amarynkeus, and his sons offered the prizes in honour of the king' (*Iliad* 23. 630–1), which included wrestling, boxing, a foot race, the 'contest of the spear' and a chariot race. In his description of the chariot race, Homer describes the distance covered by two teams running as being 'as long a distance as that of a discus swung down from the shoulder which a strong man launches making a trial of his youth' (*Iliad* 23.431–2). In Book 8 of the *Odyssey* the games include a foot race, wrestling, a long jump, the discus and boxing in the first instance.[1] While we cannot assume that Homer intended to be the world's first sports reporter, the variation in these games is significant, and they offer a touchstone against which to measure the evidence of earlier eras.

The most spectacular event of the bygone age involved bulls.

For more than a century the general understanding of 'bull-leaping', as the basic Cretan form of sport involving bulls was called by Sir Arthur Evans, the first excavator of the Bronze Age palaces on the island of Crete, was that it was a dangerous form of tumbling. The essential routine, as Evans and others presented it, comprised teams consisting of both men and women, the roles divided by gender between male 'leapers' and their female 'spotters'. The leaper would grab the bull by its horns, and when the beast protested by moving its head up and down, would somersault onto its back and then leap off. Evans's vision of bull-leaping gained an influence well beyond the usual scholarly audience when it was taken up by Mary Renault in 1962 for her wonderful retellings of the myths connected with the legendary Athenian hero, Theseus.

The story she used was essentially this: Theseus went to Crete along with thirteen other young Athenians who were to be slain by the Minotaur, the dread offspring of the Cretan king Minos' wife Pasiphae and the bull with which she had mated. The Minotaur lived in a complex structure known as the Labyrinth which was connected to the royal palace at the city of Knossos. The Athenians were sent each year in order to appease Minos, whose wrath had been kindled by the death of his son at Athens. Theseus duly arrived, seduced Minos' daughter Ariadne, slew the Minotaur and escaped with his companions (and Ariadne, whom he abandoned on the island of Naxos). For Mary Renault, 'bull dancing' stands in for the Minotaur as a form of death sentence – the leapers and dancers who distract the bull are no better than slaves. She imagined that the performer

grasped the horns, and swung up between them, going with the bull, then he soared free. The beast was too stupid to back and wait for him. It trotted on when it felt him gone. He turned in the air, a curve as lovely as a bent bow's, and on the broad back his slim feet touched down together; then they sprang up again. He seemed not to leap, but to hang above the bull, like a dragonfly over the reeds, while it ran out from under him. Then he came down to earth, feet still together, and lightly touched the catcher's hands with his, like a civility; he had no need of steadying.[2]

This varies from the views of Arthur Evans only in so far as Evans thought that the bull-leapers were Cretans of the upper class (and were supposed to live).

An important feature of Evans's reconstruction of the sport is that the performers were both male and female, gender being indicated in the frescoes that provided a significant portion of his evidence by their use of different colours to represent the various performers. In his view, males were painted in a reddish hue, while women were shown in white. To reinforce this position, when his artist restored one of the most important frescoes illustrating the sport he arranged the arms of one of the white figures so as to reveal a breast. Re-examination of the evidence has eliminated the breast, and strongly suggests that the different palettes for the performers indicated different roles rather than genders. It also suggests that Evans seriously misunderstood what he was looking at and what was humanly possible. Furthermore, he seems not to have seen an angry bull in action – irate bulls wave their heads from side to side, as anyone who's seen the running of the bulls at Pamplona is aware.

The evidence, which includes impressions on seal rings and some models as well as frescoes, depicts a variety of actions with a bull. They can be divided between depictions of the spectacular handstand and what may be either images of people failing at the handstand and falling off the bull, or making deliberate jumps across its flanks, and depictions of people grasping the horns in what might be like the rodeo sport of steer-wrestling – when a cowboy tries to bring an animal down by controlling its head. Another version, attested in northern Greece more than a thousand years after the end of the palaces on Crete and in Greece, involved killing the beast by twisting its neck. A spectacular discovery at the ancient city of Avaris at the northeastern edge of the Nile Delta in the early 1990s, and careful work restoring a variety of frescoes from Knossos, have helped put all of this evidence in a new perspective.[3]

Avaris was the capital of a people whom the Egyptians termed the Hyksos, outsiders from Palestine and northern parts who had dominated northern Egypt for several centuries before they were defeated and their capital captured by the pharaoh Ahmose I, around 1500 BC. In the wake of the conquest his son, Tuthmose III, built a palace for himself at Avaris, and there he married a princess from Crete. She brought with her (according to the most probable reconstruction) some artists who decorated a court in her new home with images from the old one – images of bull-leaping. Then something went wrong. The painting was soon stripped from the wall and deposited in a dump, from which modern archaeologists recovered it, piece by piece, and were able to reconstruct eight images of bulls with their leapers. We see here some men who have succeeded in doing a handstand, one who seems to be descending from a height over the horns of a beast, some who have fallen by the side and others who are wrestling with the animal. Another recent study of frescoes from Knossos has revealed more men coming off animals, and doing so in such a way as to make it quite clear that a person hoping to do a handstand on the back of a bull would likely be tossed on by a spotter from the rear of the animal. People seen near the bulls' horns all seem to be wrestlers.

The spread of these depictions is significant – all but one on the mainland come from palatial sites, and on Crete evidence for the activity is concentrated at Knossos. Even the representations of bull-leapers appearing on objects such as seal rings appear to have their origin in workshops located in the immediate vicinity of a palace. The location of objects connected with bull-baiting suggests very strongly that the activity shown in these frescoes was intimately connected with ideas of royalty in Crete and on the mainland.[4]

What was the ideal end to a session with a bull, or – if we may draw this conclusion from the fact that the Avaris mosaics show several beasts – with bulls? The best evidence for bull sport that does not come from frescoes tends to come from seals, the intricately carved stones that were used to close documents as a form of personal signature. One of these shows what is evidently an exhausted bull resting its head on a platform, while a leaper dives on him. More ominously, a seal from Hagia Triada on Crete shows a man spearing the bull. That theme also appears on a seal from Syria, which raises a problem of interpretation. On one view, the Haghia Triada stone combined with the Syrian evidence would suggest that bull sport in Crete was intended to end with the death of the bull. On another view, the seal stone may have been carved by an artist who was educated in the Syrian tradition, and may also represent a regional tradition. The earliest evidence for the history of bull-leaping is on a vase that comes from Hüseyindebe in central Turkey and is connected with the Hittites around 1700 BC, with whom we know Crete was then in contact. The vase shows a group of musicians playing, while one acrobat appears to be starting a handstand on the back of a bull and another to be leaping off. While the artist may have lacked the skill to represent a charging bull, the beast looks as if he is a trained member of the team. Cretan bulls – at least as far as we can tell from the way they are depicted (always dappled) – appear to have been domestic animals. Were they too trained to play their part? The fact that the Hagia Triada seal appears to be eccentric within a Cretan context would suggest that it should not be taken as offering decisive proof that the bulls were killed.[5]

In Syria it appears that bulls symbolized opposition to the order imposed by gods whose symbols were lions; but in the Hittite realm of Turkey they do not seem to have played this role. In Egypt bulls were, in places, worshipped as manifestations of divinity, and, while bull sport is attested, it tends to involve bulls fighting each other for mastery rather than against humans. Indeed, inscriptions commemorating a victorious bull in Egypt might assimilate it to the divine Apis bull. In a spell seeking to assure good luck for a dead man passing to the Underworld the deceased is compared to bulls such as the 'Lord of Herakleopolis, exalted of jewels, beautiful of feathers, K_3-bull who copulates with females'. Elsewhere it is clear that the 'K_3-bull' was the dominant animal, who proved himself in contest with other bulls and was a symbol of leadership.[6] The fact that bulls are represented only on Crete, at Knossos, suggests a close connection between sport and kingship, and the fact that the sport could be represented in Egypt suggests perhaps that the treatment of the bull had more in common with Egyptian practice, and possibly that of the Hittites, than with that of Syria.

A further question that arises in the context of bull-leaping – one to which we will be returning time and again – is that of the status of the performers. It is interesting that in the one depiction of bull sport that we find in the context of other activities – a fragmentary rhyton (a large stone vessel used for pouring libations) dating from around 1500 BC from Haghia Triada – it is keeping company with displays of violent sports. The conical rhyton contains four registers of illustration. In the top register five or six male figures have survived out of an original ten, arranged in five pairs; of these, two pairs appear to be fighting, while the other three pairs seem to be cheering them on. The second register shows three bulls, one with a leaper falling at its hooves, another with a leaper achieving a handstand, and the third between its horns. On the third and fourth registers there are three pairs of boxers (wearing headdresses) in which one man is clearly victorious over the other. It is very hard to know what to make of all this. At first sight, throwing oneself over the top of a bull may not seem to be much like punching your fellow man in the face or trying to pin him to the ground. So should they be together at all? The pugilists are shown in a very different way from the young boys depicted in one of the best (and hence most often reproduced) works of second-millennium BC Aegean art. This is a fresco from the island of Santorini showing two boys boxing, each with a glove on only one hand. Perhaps the one thing that can be said about them is that they appear to represent two teams, and that may be what they have in common with the bull-leapers, whose sport is also depicted as a team event in that people within a group seem to have had very different routines.[7]

Arthur Evans thought that people who engaged in bull sport were members of upper-class Cretan society. His view is supported in more recent work by stress on the attire of bull acrobats who wear bracelets and ankle rings, which tend to be the appurtenances of rich Cretans. It is not an unreasonable view, but nor is it alto-gether probable. On Evans's model we would then imagine potentially senior members of the court putting themselves at risk with wild animals, and without a weapon. On the whole I suspect that bull performers wore the dress of the wealthy not because they were themselves members of a governing group, but rather because they were the preferred entertainers of that group. That might qualify as one definition of 'high-status individuals' but, if it does, it will only be with the caveat that there are various ways in which one can arrive at this definition.

In the realms of Crete's neighbours, both boxing and wrestling are well attested, and both appear very much in the context of entertainments for a king – the most likely scenario for bull-leaping and, by extension, for other sports on Crete (and possibly the mainland). The view that the Haghia Triada rhyton might represent a team sport could be supported, for instance, by the fact that there seems to be some sort of team combat sport in the realm of the Hittite kings in Anatolia, staged to represent a great past victory, and that athletic events seem otherwise to have been connected with religious festivals. Egyptian pharaohs watched their subjects engage in displays of wrestling and stick fighting, and wrestling seems to have been a royal entertainment from Mesopotamia as well, where it is found as early as the third millennium BC, and as far as Syria. The story in the Book of Genesis of Jacob wrestling with God is just one of a number of instances where wrestling features in encounters between men and gods in the Semitic world, which ran from the borders of Palestine through Syria to southern Iraq. Indeed, it is quite significant that every major group in the Bronze Age, irrespective of ethnicity, offers some evidence for physical entertainments. In all these cases, however, the proof that we have places the entertainment in a framework dominated by the king – the athletes may be well rewarded for their services, but their performances are at the discretion of royal authority. On some Sumerian texts dating to before 2000 BC we can even see evidence for athletes being 'on staff' at the temple and with their own house, and while that is very early (making it unwise to generalize to practices in other Near Eastern realms), no later period suggests that performers were independent agents. Only the king was allowed to express his domination through independent demonstrations of his superior physicality.[8]

The great eastern kingdoms of the Bronze Age were societies in which physical entertainments occurred, but they were not societies that supported an independent sports culture. That there should be parallels between entertainments on Crete and in the Near East is scarcely surprising since we know that there was continuous contact between Cretans and their eastern neighbours, nor would it be entirely surprising if the Cretans imitated some of the behaviours of the more powerful courts in Egypt and the Near East. Indeed, as we have already seen in the case of Homer, it is quite likely that some elements of Anatolian (specifically Luwian) storytelling traditions entered the Greek tradition before Homer's time, just as, in Homer's generation, new stories about the gods were making their way into Greek conceptions of the divine from the Near East. These stories would establish a new paternity for Aphrodite, or make it clear that the great god Zeus kept his power through defeating a dread monster named Typhon.

In Greece as well, we can see evidence that the sporting tradition of Crete, whose palaces were earlier than those on the mainland, was incorporated into life around the palaces. There is, for instance, a fresco found in a house at Mycenae that shows bull-leaping, and on a *larnax* (plural, *larnakes*; a terracotta urn to contain the ashes of a dead person) from Tanagra in Boeotia there is a picture of bull-leaping on one side, and either boxing or armed combat on the other. The fact that other parts of the Tanagra *larnax* include a procession of weeping women and chariots may suggest that what we have here is a representation of funeral games. The problem is that Tanagra is the only site in mainland Greece where *larnakes* are used, and cremation is attested as a regular form of disposal, which would suggest that what we see here was highly unusual.[9] This may be correct, for it is also the only representation of 'physical entertainment' in these years that is devoid of an expressly palatial context. Is it also significant that it comes from the very end of the palatial period?

In any event, the most important point that may emerge from the Bronze Age evidence is that we cannot actually say there is a direct connection between what we see here and what we read later in Homer. People did box, wrestle and leap over bulls at various places, and at various times. There is also a limited number of ways in which they might actually do these things – boxing inevitably involves one person punching another, wrestling will inevitably involve one person trying to physically control the movement of another. It is most likely that a boxer wishing to win quickly will hit an opponent in the face, and that a wrestler will proceed either by lifting the opponent or by controlling his legs. What we do not see anywhere other than Greece, and then only at the very end of the Mycenaean period, is the extraction of physical entertainment from a royal to a popular context. That we also see representations of chariot-racing in this period may indicate that the status of the participants was rising outside the entertainment world. If rich people owned chariots and chariots are racing, it is likely that rich people are directly involved.

The value of the Tanagra *larnax* that depicted the bull-leaping is largely symbolic. It suggests that towards the end of the period of palatial government, changes were taking place in the realm of entertainment. Most obviously, games around funerals involving an elaborate cremation were appearing. But were they like the games in the twenty-third book of the *Iliad*? If entertainment had continued to be under the control of centralized royal regimes it is unlikely that the free-wheeling games described by Homer could have come into being. What we learn from the rest of the Bronze Age evidence is that there were earlier precedents for most of the games in Homer, as well as games that did not survive into the tradition. It is by returning to the principle we began with earlier – the comparison of what Homer has to say with tendencies in the archaeological record of the post-Mycenaean age – that we can explore the origins of the athletic tradition as we know it in Western sport – that is, an athletic tradition revolving around the respective interests of sponsors (owners), audiences and athletes.

3

Homer and Sport

The great funeral that preceded the construction of the funeral mound at Lefkandi may be seen as either a symbolic last gasp of the palatial age or the opening act of a new era. Although we have no texts to illuminate the early centuries of this era, the archaeology from roughly 1100 to 750 BC suggests that the hierarchical divisions of the palatial age had become truly a thing of the past. Power was not concentrated in the hands of bureaucrats in a central location, but diffused throughout the small communities that now dominated the Greek landscape. Leaders of this society may have been the descendants of those worthies who had once held the position of *qu-si-re-u* in the tablets of the palatial period.[1] In the Homeric world, following the rules of sound shifts in the development of the Greek language, *qu* was now pronounced *ba* and *re* as *le*, as the word was now *basileus* (pl. *busileis*). In later Greek the term would be applied to monarchs like the great king of Persia, but at this point it continued to designate the local boss. A *basileus* was most decidedly not a monarchical *wanax* – in what may be one of the many recollections of the Mycenaean age in the tradition that Homer knew, Alcinous on Phaeacia controlled ten *basileis* – and the 'heroes' of Homer who support the *wanax* Agamemnon are themselves *basileis*. They determined what was just and unjust amongst the people who followed them, and they led them in war. How well they performed these functions is open to question. Homer's slightly younger contemporary, Hesiod, complained of the 'gift-devouring *basileis*' who corrupted the justice of the gods. That said, it was at the funeral of a *basileus* in Euboea named Amphidamas that Hesiod is said to have enjoyed his greatest moment of glory, winning a singing contest (later legend had it that he defeated Homer himself).

The *mise-en-scène* of Hesiod's triumph would thus be an event like that described by Homer in Book 23 of the *Iliad* but with some additional elements (again a reminder that there was no one way that such events could unfold). If we follow Homer's model, there would have been a single sponsor responsible for ensuring that the events took place in an orderly fashion. This included proper announcement and exhibition of the prizes (in Homer's world there were prizes for losers as well as for winners in most events), announcement of the competitors (in Homer, this was simply the self-presentation of the competitors to the audience), announcement of the rules governing the event, adjudication of disputes and disposition of the prizes.[2]

While Homer's description of what happened within a set of games will be readily recognizable as providing the framework for many later contests, it is in the language of his description of these games, rather than in the list of events, that we have our most important evidence for the transformation of physical entertainment into true sport. For, although the atmosphere of the games in the *Iliad* and the *Odyssey* may feel quite similar – people of high status competing with each other to gain further recognition – the two sets of games differ in quite significant ways. In the *Iliad* there is no suggestion that anyone who is not of high status would ever compete, while in the *Odyssey* the contestants are simply described

as 'many and worthy young men', including three sons of Alcinous.[3]
One of those sons asks Odysseus to join in the games with words
redolent of a world that has not experienced the brutality of war;
beginning what will become an exploration of the nature of fame,
he says:

> Come, friend, have a go at the games, if you have skill in any, for it is
> good for you to know sports, for a man has no greater fame than that
> which he acquires with his feet or his hands. (*Odyssey* 8.145–9)

Odysseus turns down this offer, at which point Euryalos, 'equal to
Ares, the destroyer of men' and the victor in wrestling, challenges
Odysseus with the words:

> Stranger, I do not judge you to be like a man skilled in sports such
> as are played by men in many places, but to be like a man plying
> his trade in a ship with many oars, a leader of sailors and those who
> are traders, mindful of the outgoing cargo and on the lookout for one
> to take home, and greedy profits; you are not suitable for games.
> (*Odyssey* 8.159–64)

The implication is that even if Odysseus might actually have been
the sort of man who sailed the seas as a merchant, he could still
pass for the right sort of character if he showed that he was good
at the games. Here Odysseus is a genuine hero, and proves that
he is good at games in quite a spectacular way, making it possible (at the beginning of the next book) to lay claim to his true
identity. There is no such ambiguity in the *Iliad*, where Epeios,
the man who would later design the Trojan horse, stands forth
to say:

Let whomsoever of the Achaeans will take away the two-handled
goblet come forward; I say that none other of the Achaeans, winning
in boxing, will take away the mule, since I declare that I am the best.
It is enough that I am lacking in battle, for it could not be ever that
a man could be a master of all things. I will say this straight out, and
this will be as a thing accomplished, that I will smash his flesh with
a straight blow, and I will shatter his bones. Let his kinsmen stand
by together, waiting, and they will take him away, defeated by my
hand. (*Iliad* 23.667–75)

It is perhaps disappointing to the modern taste that Epeios makes
good on his promise, defeating his rival with a single blow. But the
crucial point here is that he uses his success as an athlete to assert
his place amongst the great. Somewhat earlier, Nestor had done
much the same thing, reminding all who would listen of the glory
that he had won at the games earlier in his life. There is a subtle
difference here between the treatment of sport in the fully heroic
world and that in the ideal world of the gentle Phaeacians. This is
perhaps to be expected in a poet whose works represent an age in
transition. What is also significant is that in both cases the athletes
are claiming high status because of their skill as athletes, and re-
inforcing that status through success. There is no known parallel
in the Near East, or real reason to think that this had been true of
the palatial age.

There are two further moments in this book that reveal very different views about the role of the man who is in charge of the
games. Do these reflect disputes that occurred even as Homer was
singing? The question at the heart of these passages is who deter-
mines the victor? At the very end of the book, Agamemnon stands
forth to compete in the contest of spear-throwing. At that point
Achilles stops the event and proclaims him the winner, while urging

that he allow the object set out as the first prize (a spear) to be given to Meriones, who will thereby finish second (but presumably will mind less if he gets the more valuable object). Such an act is not the forerunner of the later Greek custom whereby a competitor could resign in the face of a superior opponent, allowing him the honour of winning 'without sand'. It is simply an autocratic act by the man in charge, recognizing the political power of a contestant. Agamemnon sees the gesture for what it is and duly passes the first prize on to his erstwhile opponent.

The 'victory' of Agamemnon stands in stark contrast to the fight that had erupted over the distribution of prizes in the chariot race held earlier in the *Iliad*. By far the longest of the events that Homer describes, the race began with five teams, and was supposed to run as one lap on a course whose starting line was located on an old road at one end of which stood Achilles, and at the other an old tree at a crossroads, where Achilles had stationed a valued henchman to make sure that all the chariots rounded it properly. The chariots are driven by Eumelus (who crashes), Menelaus, the brother of Agamemnon (and sometime spouse of Helen), Antilochus, the son of Nestor, Diomedes, one of the very greatest heroes, and Meriones, a man much less important than the others. Diomedes wins the race, but Achilles is tempted at the end to offer the prize for second place to Eumelus. As he stands to give the prizes, Achilles says:

> The best man brings in his single-hoofed horses in last place. Come, let us give him second prize as is fitting; the son of Tydeus [Diomedes] will carry off the first prize. (*Iliad* 23.536–8)

As he speaks, the audience is inclined to agree with him. Ancient commentators on this scene understood it to mean that Achilles recognized Eumelus was the best driver, and felt that a man should not be deprived of honour by ill-fortune. Perhaps that is so. But it is also true that on such a reading, there is no point in having a competition if you can decide in advance who will triumph. It is the angry Antilochus who then says that actual results must be allowed to count, and opposes what may be seen as a view of sport based on perceived virtue with one based upon achievement. In so doing he states the rationale for sport as we now understand it:

> Achilles, I will be very angry with you if you do what you say. You wish to take away the prize, thinking that his chariot and the swift horses broke down, but that he is a worthy man; but he ought to have prayed to the immortal gods, which is why he comes in last of all. If you are sad and there is friendship in you for him, there is a lot of gold in your tent and there is bronze and there are beasts, there are serving girls and single-footed horses, take one of these and give him an even greater prize than mine, and do it now so that the Achaeans will applaud you. I will not give up this mare, if someone wishes to make a fuss about this, let him fight me with his hands. (*Iliad* 23.543–54)

Antilochus' speech asserts the point that the prize is a mark of honour, as it represents the victory. It does not matter if Achilles wishes to give Eumelus a valuable gift on his own account as a token of his affection (and it will turn out that he does). What matters to Antilochus is that he should receive what he has earned; he may have been an underdog, but he raced a better race, and Eumelus got what he deserved for his excessive confidence (he really should have prayed to the gods for his achievement). People might want to place bets, as they do in this race, or they might want to handicap it, but even the great Achilles, the man who set the prizes for the contest, cannot influence the results.

The contrast between the emotion in Antilochus' speech and the action of Achilles in dealing with Agamemnon is a sign of a tradition in transformation. The fact that Achilles would intervene one more time to settle a result – he halts the wrestling match between Odysseus and Telemonian Ajax at one fall apiece (victory should have gone to the man who won two out of three) – is a sign that the tradition could be deeply conflicted. Homer's audience would have recognized the symbolism of the contest between the crafty Odysseus and the massive Ajax and, if they were well versed in the tradition, they would also have acknowledged that this match might prefigure a later episode. For after the death of Achilles the Greeks held a contest to see who should inherit his arms – Odysseus, who carried Achilles' body from the fray, or Ajax who protected his back. Odysseus was declared the winner of that contest and Ajax, feeling cheated, went mad. But the literary aspects of Achilles' decision to halt the match when the two were evenly ranked is less significant for our purposes than the fact that Homer thought his readers would accept the device he uses to end the match – the simple fiat of the man who was administering the games.[4]

Obviously the games in the twenty-third book of the *Iliad* never happened, but Homer's decision to include these incidents as a way of moving his plot forward is potentially an indication of the importance of athletic competition in marking points of transition. Funeral games are not just about saying farewell to the dead; they may also enable the survivors to reintegrate without the vital presence of the person whose departure they are lamenting. So it is that in Homer's narrative, the games look ahead to other aspects of the story. Achilles smiles when Antilochus lectures him on the awarding of prizes, and this reminds us that Antilochus became close to Achilles in his last days. Odysseus would later defeat Ajax in the contest for possession of Achilles' arms, and the reconciliation with Agamemnon marks an important moment in the *Iliad*, as Achilles shows that he has put aside the anger that motivated him for so long, making it believable that he might actually be able to see old King Priam of Troy as a human being.

The *Iliad* ends with the funeral games for Hector, after Priam has come in secret to the tent of Achilles to retrieve the body of his son. Achilles is moved by thoughts of his own father (whom he now knows he will never see again) to feel sympathy for the Trojan king and share a moment of profound grief in what remains one of the most powerful passages in Western literature. That said, literary devices are viable only if they reflect events or practices that the audience can recognize as legitimate or plausible. In later Greek sport and, indeed, in the *Odyssey*, the sorts of interventions that Homer depicts would have been unthinkable. They cannot be seen as a vision of the future (though they may be seen rather as reflections of Homer's own time), but more plausibly they echo tales about other games that the tradition had preserved through the centuries. Autocratic decisions about prizes and victory are markers of a world where a king could decide who won or who deserved the prize. It is not the choice of specific events that makes Book 23 of the *Iliad* a sign of the burgeoning new world. It is precisely the speech of Antilochus, the statement that prizes should follow actual results, that reveals the tension that might still have been in the air.

Homer not only shows us something of the atmosphere that surrounded the games, he may also reveal a little more of the way that they were held in these years. His audience cannot seem to envision a world where there are properly prepared grounds for athletics. When Alcinous announces that it is time for the games at Phaeacia, he presides over events that are held in the Agora, or market-place, of his city. No temple is mentioned, no sacrifices precede the events,

31

which follow a grand feast to which the lords of the land are invited, while the common people (lots of them) gather to watch the games. The need to make use of what one has on hand, in the case of funeral games, appears very strongly in the games for Patroclus. The race-track is defined by the line of an old road and a solitary tree that stands at a crossroads. The riders strain to keep their horses inside the line, and in doing so must also avoid 'a break in the ground in which the winter water gathered and dug out the road' (*Iliad* 23. 419–20). In one of the most memorable scenes in the book, the line of the foot race runs too close to the altars where Achilles sacrificed the animals for Patroclus. In the gore and dung left after the slaughter of the beasts the goddess Athena causes the leader to slip and fall, giving the victory to her favourite, Odysseus. Finally, of course, the intervention of the gods needed to be accounted for. As Antilochus said, Eumelus should have prayed to the immortal gods if he really wanted to win. That is what Diomedes did when he saw that Apollo had made him drop his whip at the beginning of the race (Athena gave it back to him) and it was to Athena that Odysseus prayed to gain his victory in the foot race. Here at least the immortal represents the element of uncertainty, of chance and simple luck that could make a man into a champion. The immortal gods would always be welcome at the games, even when the voice of an autocratic sponsor was silenced.[5]

Looking ahead to the later development of Greek sport, there are two further aspects of the games in Homer that signify a transitional age. The first is simply the absence of any notion of a calendar. In the fullness of time, games would be linked with religious festivals throughout the Greek world but, for Homer, there is no such need. It was only within his probable lifetime that Greek states were beginning to develop regular institutions, of which a formal civic calendar was a crucial feature. Once these institutions had come into being, it would become feasible regularly to institute games and separate them from the fiat of an individual like Alcinous, or the chance demise of an aristocrat. The absence of a regular schedule invariably limited participation to people from nearby areas, given that funeral games needed to be held shortly after an individual's death. The point of the games that Alcinous provided was to enable Odysseus to tell the tale of how glorious were the accomplishments of the Phaeacians at such events.

The second significant aspect of the Homeric games is that the heroes are all clothed. In the classical period, nudity was a defining characteristic of the Greek athlete and set Greek athletic events apart from those of other peoples. Even those who may have watched Greek athletes competing (such as the Etruscans in Italy) would not later adopt the practice of performance in the nude. The rise of the calendar and the departure of clothing are two important aspects of the rise of athletic culture in the generations after Homer.

PART 2

Olympia

4

From Myth to History[1]

Pindar was a poet who became famous because he wrote poems about the famous. His subjects were people who won at one or another of the four great athletic festivals of his time, the fifth century BC. Pindar was thus composing some three hundred years after Homer sang the *Iliad*. He lived in a world where writing was well established (if not widely used) and where the city-state (*polis*) was the primary form of social organization.

Despite these differences, Homer remained important. The Greek conception of history included the Trojan War as an actual event, and the Greek sense of identity drew heavily upon the mythological tradition that Homer and Hesiod represented. It was this tradition that shaped definitions of what it was to be Greek as opposed to 'foreign' (the Greek word was *barbaros*) and the sense that there were things that 'all Greeks could do' and that only Greeks could do. Most important in this regard seems to have been participation in the highly developed athletic community that had grown up around the four great, or 'Panhellenic' ('all-Greece'), festivals. It would be in Pindar's lifetime that a king of Macedon in northern Greece, Alexander, would have to prove his 'Greek' credentials through appeal to mythic ancestors from the Peloponnese so that he could compete at one of these festivals. It was also perhaps natural that when Pindar and others wrote about figures of the present, they did so by placing their deeds in the broad context of the mythic past while asserting that their praise of those deeds was true to the event.[2]

Myth also lay behind the Panhellenic festivals, which brought people together from all over the region. These festivals were the Olympic, Pythian, Nemean and Isthmian games, and were held according to a fixed four-year cycle. It began with the Olympics, which honoured the god Zeus at his shrine in Elis, a state in the northwestern Peloponnese. The Pythian games were held every four years at the great oracular shrine of the god Apollo at Delphi – in any given cycle, these took place two years after the Olympics. The Nemean games took place at the shrine of Zeus at Nemea in Argos (the leading state of the northeastern Peloponnese), falling between the Pythian and Olympic years; the Isthmian games honouring Poseidon, god of the sea, were held outside Corinth (the most important state in the northern Peloponnese) in the same years as the Olympic or Pythian games, with the proviso that the Isthmian games should be celebrated in May–June. The Pythian and Olympic games were always held in July–August.

Probably born in 518 at the city of Chaeronea in Boeotia (central Greece), Pindar lived to a very great age – tradition has it that he died in 443 BC, and the evidence of his poetry (which spans the period from 498 to 446 BC) suggests that tradition is reasonably sound. The potential problem with this supposition is not simply that no Greek in the time of Pindar could have dated anything in conjunction with an event that would happen hundreds of years in the future (the birth of Christ); it is also that there was no common way of measuring time in the Greek world. Our ability now to determine the date for an event in the lifetime of Pindar depends on being able to synchronize that event with a list of magistrates at the city of Athens, the eponymous archons who gave their names to an official year that ran roughly from midsummer to midsummer. At the end of the fourth century BC, the list of Athenian archons was correlated with a list of victors at the Olympic games in an effort to provide a common chronology for the Greek world. This world had, by then, been massively expanded by another king of Macedon, also named Alexander, who had conquered the great power of Pindar's day, the Persian Empire, to lay the foundation of Greek kingdoms that would extend as far east as Afghanistan. During this period the Greek heartland consisted of what we now recognize as the central and southern regions of modern Greece, portions of southern Italy, Sicily, western Turkey and Cyprus.

The fact that the chronological system based on Athenian archons and Olympic years did not achieve any sort of currency until more than a century after Pindar's death makes it very difficult to know whether early synchronisms are legitimate. Pindar himself gives no indication that he would have placed his own birth in the second year of the sixty-second Olympiad, and he would almost certainly have objected to hearing that he was born in the archonship of Habron at Athens (518 BC). He died three years after the archonship of Callimachus (446 BC), when the Athenians had been evicted from his homeland after thirteen years of promoting the extreme form of democracy that they practised in their own city. Pindar was no fan of democracy, which he regarded as the despotism of the masses. Even if he did once write a poem in honour of Athens, his preferred subjects were the very rich, and he had a tendency to write for people who fell outside the Athenian ambit. Many of his clients came from the island of Aegina, which would have been visible in Pindar's day to the south of Athens, and had a long history of hostility to that city which culminated in the eviction of its population in 431 (to be replaced by Athenians).[3]

The complexity of Greek dating systems and the way that a person in the age of Pindar would have thought about time is directly relevant to the history of sport. If we accept the date for the first celebration of the Olympic games that would emerge in the generation after Pindar died, then in 776 BC, perhaps a generation before Homer, there was a festival attached to a temple in northwestern Greece that drew people from all over Greece to watch a foot race. We would also have to accept that Hippias of Elis, who compiled the list of victors, had access to lists of winners that were made when people were not generally keeping accounts of that sort.[4] It may not be comforting that most of what we know about Hippias derives from the pen of Plato, whose memorable portrait of the man reveals an amazingly pompous 'public intellectual' whose pretensions were scarcely matched by his actual knowledge.

Doubts aside, the history of the Olympics as Hippias reconstructed it is not simply a chronological exercise, but one in creating the history of sport. This history is based on the dates at which new competitions were admitted to the games (or when prizes were first awarded for these competitions). The first Olympiad consisted simply of a sprint of roughly two hundred metres or, in Greek terms, a stade – hence the name *stadion* for the race, and ultimately for the building in which the race took place – won by a man named Coroebus. At the fourteenth celebration of the games (720 BC) a prize was also awarded for a foot race that was double the length of the first – the *diaulos*, which means 'double course' – and at the fifteenth (716 BC) for a distance race, the *dolichos* or 'long course'. At the eighteenth celebration (708) there were two new events, the pentathlon, which consisted of competition in the discus, the javelin, the long jump, a *stadion* race and a wrestling match; and a separate wrestling event (pentathletes did not normally compete in the regular *stadion* or wrestling championships).

In the twenty-third Olympiad (688) boxing was added, and the four-horse chariot race, the *tethrippon*, in the twenty-fifth (680). In 648 prizes for a horse race as well as pancration – a combination of boxing and wrestling – were added. Events for boys in a foot race, wrestling, pentathlon (immediately discontinued) and boxing were added in the thirty-seventh, thirty-eighth and forty-first Olympiads (632, 628 and 616). The games that Pindar knew were rounded out with the introduction of a race in armour (Olympiad sixty-five, 520), as well as races for mule carts and mares whose riders would run alongside them in armour for the last lap (the seventieth and seventy-first Olympiads, 500 and 496 respectively, both events discontinued in 444).

Hippias' elaborate history did not convince other learned Greeks of his time. The great historian Herodotus, whose probable birth date was about forty years after Pindar's, knew a considerable amount about sports heroes but he does not refer to any numbered Olympiad. Thucydides, who was writing his history of the Peloponnesian war at the time that Hippias produced his list, had no use for it; he prided himself on being able to recognize a fake when he saw it, and disparaging comments on Hippias' project may be read into a couple of lines of Thucydides' history.[5]

If Hippias' list was unconvincing when he produced it, was that because he manifestly made it all up? Or was there some sort of evidence, some sort of earlier tradition upon which he could draw, and was the criticism of his project simply that he went beyond the bounds of this tradition? Is it, for instance, possible that Pindar knew that some people thought that Coroebus won the *stadion* at the first Olympics, or had some inkling of a local tradition that Hippias would later employ? The answers are 'yes', 'probably' and 'maybe'.

The reason for answering these questions in such an indecisive way is that there is not a lot of evidence, and what there is tends to be ambiguous. The most important piece of evidence is a treaty between two Sicilian cities that was inscribed on a bronze tablet around 500 BC. Just as the document breaks off we can read the words, 'the ones who fled before this agreement [unknown number of words missing] these are not to be bound by the oath, neither these ones nor those who fled with them; this year of the Olympiad [break in the bronze with an indication of an aspirated letter] begins these [agreements]'. If the aspirated letter here was the first letter of a number, that could only be 'six' in Greek (*hex*), possibly in some such formulation as *hexkaidekatas*, or 'sixteenth'. This might yield a significant date – if we accept the suggestion offered by one scholar that the events here can be dated to the 480s, rather than 500 then the sixteenth Olympiad would indicate a succession of Olympiads that extended back in time to around 550, thought neither this date, nor one counting backwards from 500 is important in Hippias' tradition. Although it is tempting to assert that this inscription proves that the games began in the mid-sixth century, we would, in doing so, be doing exactly what Hippias did – piling the hypothetical upon the questionable to create a mound of pseudo-information. In fact the understanding of the reference to an Olympiad in this document might not be remotely correct. Other texts of the period include dating formulae such as 'the alliance will be a hundred years and begin in this year', which makes it possible that what the author was trying to say was that this agreement was reached in an Olympiad year. This would simply mean that people thought it was significant that something had happened in an Olympic year. We know that this was the case at another city in Sicily, which held a special purification ceremony every four years when news that the games were to be held reached the city.[6]

If we do not have direct evidence for a coherent Elean system of numbering Olympiads, this still does not mean that they did not have their own traditions – the tomb of Coroebus might already have been visible on the borders of their territory, and associated with the games. That there should already be controversy on the 'true story' of the games in Pindar's time would seem to emerge from his poem celebrating the victory of Hagesidamus, a youth from Locris in southern Italy who won the boys' boxing in 476 BC. In this poem he tells how Hercules set up the games 'with six altars near the tomb of Pelops'. Here:

> The valiant son of Zeus gathered the whole army and all the plunder [they had just destroyed an evil king of Elis and his folk] at Pisa and measured the hallowed grove for his great father. He fenced round the Altis [Santuary] in the open, and set it aside; he made the surrounding plain a resting place for the evening meal, honouring the stream of the Alpheus [the river that ran by the grounds at Olympia] along with the twelve ruling gods; and he named the hill of Kronos, for previously it had no name, for when Oenomaeus ruled it was covered with much snow. The Fates stood close by at the newly brought-forth festival, and Time, the sole guarantor of truth, who, going forward revealed clearly how, dividing up the spoils of war, [Hercules] offered up the finest parts and founded the four-year festival with the first Olympiad and its victors. (Pindar *Olympian Odes* 10.43–59)[7]

Pindar duly goes on to name those victors, including a man named Oionos as the winner of the *stadion*. It is hard not to read the reference to Time as the guarantor of truth as suggesting that traditions involving other people were simply false. The foundation of the games by someone who was not from Elis could be important in an era of controversy, as the age of Pindar was. If the games were those founded by Hercules, then they could truly be thought to belong to all Greeks, and thus be open to all Greeks. In 476 BC that is a very important thing to be clear about.

The poem is one of two celebrating Hagesidamus' victory in that year, and Hagesidamus is one of three of Pindar's clients. The others were two of the most powerful men in the Greek world – Hieron and Theron. Their passion was horse-racing; their jobs were dominating Greek cities. Hieron was tyrant of Syracuse, the most important Greek city on Sicily; Theron was tyrant of Agrigentum, on the south coast of the same island, and often Hieron's rival. In addition to Pindar's poems we have one by the poet Bacchylides of Ceos, who wrote at considerable length to honour the victory of Hieron. The term 'tyrant' in both cases designated a man who was in charge of a city; it did not yet have the later Greek (and modern) connotation of a brute exercising unconstitutional power.[8] Pindar's poem for Hieron also tells a story about the early history of the games, of how young Pelops asked his former lover, the god Poseidon, for aid in winning a chariot race against a rebarbative king of Elis, Oenomaeus, who offered his daughter Hippodameia in marriage to whoever could defeat him in a chariot race. Thirteen had already tried, failed, and been killed. Poseidon helped, Pelops won, Oenomaeus died (though not obviously in Pindar's poem), and the happy couple had six children.

The remarkable concentration of surviving texts surrounding the Olympic games of 476 – more than for any other year – is perhaps testimony not only to the enormous personalities of Hieron and Theron, but also to the momentous events that had occurred at the time of the previous Olympiad. The year 480 BC had seen the threatened destruction of Greek independence throughout the Mediterranean world. In that year Theron had joined forces with Gelon (Hieron's elder brother) to resist an effort by the Carthaginians to take over the Greek cities of Sicily. Carthage was a powerful city on the coast of modern Tunisia that had been founded some three hundred years earlier by people from the city of Tyre in modern Lebanon (then known as Phoenicia). Greek settlers had begun moving west at about the same time, and relations between the two peoples had been variously friendly or antagonistic ever since. Under the command of Gelon, the Greek forces of Sicily had crushed the Carthaginians at the battle of Himera on the north coast of the island. The base upon which a massive tripod and image of victory once stood remains at Olympia, inscribed with the words 'Gelon, the son of Deinomenes, the Syracusan, dedicated this to Apollo. Bion, the son of Diodorus, of Miletus made the tripod and the victory.' A few years later, after another battle (this time against the Etruscans of Italy), Hieron sent a helmet to Olympia inscribed with the words 'Hieron the son of Deinomenes and the Syracusans dedicated this [taken from] the Etruscans at Cumae.'9 The helmet joined other victory ornaments that adorned stakes arrayed atop the embankment around the stadium where non-equestrian events were held.

The other great event of 480 was the repulse of an invasion of mainland Greece by Xerxes, king of Persia. The Persian Empire had grown into the most powerful state on the planet under Xerxes' three predecessors. Starting in the mid-sixth century, the first great Persian king, Cyrus, had conquered much of the Near East and what is now Turkey. Cyrus' son Cambyses (before his assassination by a cabal of officers) had added Egypt to his domain; the leader of the assassins, who became known as King Darius, had solidified control over the existing empire while also expanding his reach into what is now the eastern edge of northern Greece and, at one point, the southern Ukraine. The eastern border of the empire lay in Afghanistan, its northern borders in what are now the former Soviet Republics of Kazakhstan and Turkestan.

In 499 BC, Darius' Greek subjects in western Turkey and, slightly later, Cyprus, had risen in rebellion. The people of Athens had sent twenty ships, 'the beginning of woes for the Greeks and barbarians' as Herodotus put it, to assist in the revolt. Once it had been suppressed, Darius resolved to launch a 'pre-emptive war' against the Greek terrorists who had supported the rebels – the term 'terrorist' in this case is not an overt modernizing imposition, for the stated purpose of the Persian intervention was to avenge the destruction of a famous temple. The expedition, by sea, destroyed the city of Eretria (the descendant of old Lefkandi), which had also aided the rebels, and then landed at Marathon. This was in the late summer of 490 BC, and the Athenians destroyed the expedition on the beach. Xerxes, who succeeded his father a few years later, now had two 'atrocities' to avenge in order that the regime would not lose face. So it was that, after massive preparations, he arrived in Greece in the late summer of 480 with an army and navy that may have been 150,000 strong.[10] The fleet was destroyed in a naval battle off the island of Salamis, and the next summer the army that had remained after Xerxes had fled for home was destroyed at the battle of Plataea.

The Greek states that had managed to unite against Carthage and Persia soon fell to quarrelling. Hieron nearly went to war with Theron after Gelon's death in 478.[11] At the same time Athens and Sparta, which had played the leading role in the defeat of Xerxes, were beginning to go their separate ways in disagreement over what policies to pursue. The Spartans preferred to stay at home, while the Athenians (whose city had been destroyed by Xerxes in the days before Salamis) favoured the creation of an alliance of states in the Aegean against the Persians. The situation in Greece itself was further complicated by the fact that Thebes, the leading city in Boeotia, had sided with the Persians.

For people who disagreed, or even for those sensitive to the claims of an important neighbour, Olympia and the other sites in the cycle of games were perfect locations in which to score points in the unofficial, though all-important, league table of relative clout. The Panhellenic festivals offered such a venue precisely because they were thought to go back to a neutral foundation. Each set of games had its own foundation myth that removed the original celebration from the control of any individual state.[12] There could perhaps be no greater symbol of this neutrality than the list of victors for the games in the great year 480. The list as we have it comes from a papyrus, copied in the second or third century AD, found in the city of Oxyrhynchus in Egypt. As is the way with such documents – the texts from Oxyrhynchus all come from the city's rubbish dump – the text is damaged: several letters are missing at the beginning of the left-hand side of each line, the top of the list is missing, and the first seven lines are reconstructed from other sources (words not in the text are, as elsewhere, shown within square brackets, as are the translations). But the damage is not such that we cannot see essentially what happened:

[Astylus the Syracusan won the *stadion* [sprint]
Astylus the Syracusan won the *diaulos* [double sprint]
Dromeus the Stymphalian won the *dolichos* [distance race]
Theopompus the Erean won the pentathlon
[?] won the wrestling
Theogenes of Thasos won the boxing
Dromerus the Mantinean won the pancration]
Xenopeithes the Chiot won the sprint for boys
[name lost] the Argive won the boys' wrestling
[name partially lost]phanes the Hereian won the boys' boxing
[Ast]ylus the Syracusan won the *hoplitodromos* [race in armour]

[Dai]ton and Arsilochus, the Thebans, won the *tethrippon* [four-horse chariot race]

[the Arg]ive people won the horse race. (*Oxyrhynchus Papyrus* n. 222)

The Carthaginians were advancing along the south coast of Italy and Xerxes was in northern Greece as these games were played out. The list of victors, however, reflects a powerful desire to do business as normal (or, perhaps, not to offend states that might prove to be on the winning side). Thasos and Chios were both under Persian control (Chios had provided a significant number of ships to the Persian fleet), Thebes was about to declare for Persia and Argos was refusing to join the alliance against the Persians.

As time passed, diplomacy continued to be important, if not even more so than ever. At the Isthmian and Pythian games in 478, the Greeks who had assembled there seem only to have come (or to have come primarily) from states that had joined in the war against Persia. Isthmia now had symbolic importance in the tale of resistance to the Persians; it was at the temple of Poseidon at Isthmia that the Greeks had met to determine an award for the man who had done the most in the campaign of 480. The winner was the Athenian, Themistocles. At the Pythian games, the Greeks would have seen for the first time the great serpent column that had been erected (with some controversy over the wording) by the Spartan king Pausanias, who had commanded the Greek armies at Plataea. It listed all the states that had joined in the struggle. Just before the Olympics of 476 began, Themistocles may have suggested that the assembled Greeks tear apart the sumptuous tent of Hieron's delegation and refuse to allow his horse to compete because he had not helped in the war against Persia.[13]

5

Olympia in 480 BC

In 480, just as at every celebration of the games, the athletes who expected to compete at Olympia were required to assemble in the city of Elis for a month before the opening ceremonies. It was now, as the athletes swore an oath to train properly, that the officials in charge of the games determined who should be allowed to compete, and in which categories. There were two basic categories at this point – men and boys – and contestants were placed in the appropriate category according to how they appeared to the judges (most entrants in the boys' category were between the ages of twelve and seventeen, but any boy who appeared especially well developed would be added to the men's group). At the same time the athletes had to prove that they were citizens of Greek cities and, for the events in the stadium (the foot races, the pentathlon and the combat events), that they had a chance of winning.

Almost all the evidence that we have for the procedures at the games comes from a much later period (mostly, the second century AD), but the emotions described amongst the boys who sought to be allowed to compete are timeless: 'Will I qualify? Do I have a chance? Will the officials be fair? How good is [my opponent] really?' A young man once told of his anxiety about competing by describing a dream in which he and the other boys passed before the eyes of the judges and saw that one of these judges was the god Asclepius (concerned with good health). He should not have worried about the mortal judges, as he died before he could compete.

The oath sworn by the judges at Olympia, described for us by another Pausanias, the traveller whose account of a visit to Olympia in the second century AD is a crucial source for the history of ancient sport, was part of a ceremony so antique that no one knew why part of it existed at all.[1] The judges swore that they would be fair in determining whether a contestant should compete as a boy or man, and that they would keep secret all that they knew about him. Presumably part of the inspection process comprised private displays of ability before the judges, and in the case of a new contestant, people might reasonably want to know what he could do before the day of the competition. It was up to others to determine whether a person was really Greek and met the necessary qualification of good character. The sorts of decisions that could be made at this time, and their impact, are reflected in Pausanias' tale of various contests in the boys' category, motivated by his seeing a statue of a young victor named Pherias outside the stadium at Olympia:

> . . . [in] the seventy-eighth Festival [464 BC] [Pherias] was considered very young, and, being judged to be as yet unfit to wrestle, was debarred from the contest. At the next Festival he was admitted to the boys' wrestling-match and won it. What happened to this Pherias was different; in fact the exact opposite of what happened at Olympia to Nicasylus of Rhodes. Being eighteen years of age he was not allowed by the Eleans to compete in the boys' wrestling-match, but won the men's match and was proclaimed victor. He was afterwards proclaimed victor at Nemea also and at the Isthmus. But when he was twenty years old he met his death before he returned home

to Rhodes. The feat of the Rhodian wrestler at Olympia was in my
opinion surpassed by Artemidorus of Tralles. He failed in the boys'
pancration at Olympia, the reason of his failure being his extreme
youth. When, however, the time arrived for the contest held by the
Ionians of Smyrna, his strength had so increased that he beat in the
pancration on the same day those who had competed with him at
Olympia, after the boys, the beardless youths as they are called, and
thirdly the pick of the men. His match with the beardless youths
was the outcome, they say, of a trainer's encouragement; he fought
the men because of the insult of a pancratiast in the men's division.
Artemidorus won an Olympic victory among the men at the two
hundred and twelfth Festival [AD 68]. (*Description of Greece* 6.14.1–3,
Loeb tr. adapted)

In Pausanias' view the history of sport is a continuous one
whereby one might compare achievement across the ages, even
as one might now compare the elegance of Pele with that of
Ronaldinho or the home-run power of Babe Ruth with Hank Aaron
(or even Barry Bonds). In his world, of course, this had to be done
without film – Pausanias would never have seen Artemidorus of
Tralles any more than he would have seen Pherias of Aegina.

When it came to competing, it behoved the participants to get
a sense of who was doing what. Hieron and Theron chose not to
compete in the same events, and both men appear to have awaited
news of the results at home – equestrian events were the only ones
where credit went to the owner rather than to the contestant.[2] So
it is that instead of describing the efforts of the young jockey who
rode the horse Pherenikos – the name means 'Victory-carrier' –
to victory (Greek jockeys always appear to have been young boys
who rode without benefit of either a saddle or clothing), Bacchylides wrote:

Gold-armed Dawn saw, next to the wide-eddying Alpheus, young
Pherenikos, chestnut hued and storm swift, and she saw him too at
Delphi; placing my hand upon the earth I swear that in no contest
was he dirtied by the dust of horses in front of him as he stretched
for the finish. In strength he is like the North wind, obeying his rider
as he races towards victory and new applause for Hieron. (*Victory
Odes* 5.36–50)

Pindar noted that, although absent, Theron had 'reached to the far-
thest point with his virtues, and, from his home he grasped the
pillar of Hercules with his victory' (*Olympian Odes* 3.44–5).

The situation in boxing was perhaps even more complex. The
victor in 480 was Theogenes of Thasos, who had taken the crown
from Euthymus of Locris.[3] Theogenes had tried to become the first
man ever to win both the pancration and the boxing in the same
games but, although admitted to the pancration, he had been so
exhausted by his struggle with Euthymus that he had not been able
to compete. The result was that

. . . the umpires fined Theagenes[4] a talent, to be sacred to the god,
and a talent for the harm done to Euthymus, holding that it was
merely to spite him that he entered for the boxing competition. For
this reason they condemned him to pay an extra fine privately to
Euthymus. At the seventy-sixth Festival Theagenes paid in full the
money owed to the god . . . and as compensation to Euthymus did
not enter for the boxing-match. At this Festival, and also at the next
following, Euthymus won the crown for boxing. (Pausanias *Description of Greece* 6.6.6)

The presence of Euthymus who, like Theogenes, would join those
athletes whose achievements would become the stuff of legend,

puts yet others of Pindar's compositions for 476 into perspective. This is the work honouring Hagesidamus of Locris for victory in the boys' boxing. The first of the poems for Hagesidamus might have been composed in the immediate aftermath of the victory, to grace some sort of party in or around Olympia. The second, much longer poem was written for a victory celebration at Locris some time later, according to Pindar. There is no reason to disbelieve the poet on this point, or to interpret the opening lines of the work as anything other than a clever literary conceit to cover the fact that Hagesidamus, son of Archestratus, came a distant third amongst the Pindaric clients of this year – Pindar had, after all, to celebrate the victory of Pherenikos for Hieron and, twice, the victory of Gelon. In the opening he simply says:

> Recall for me the Olympic victory of the son of Archestratus, from wherever it is written in my mind; although I owe him a sweet song, I have forgotten it. But you, o Muse, and your sister, Truth, the daughter of Zeus, with a just hand, restrain the reproach of lying and of a crime committed against a friend. (*Olympian Odes* 10.1–6)

More interesting, perhaps, would be to know why Archestratus paid for two celebrations. We may wonder if Hagesidamus did not realize that he had come to the end of his Olympic career. Now at the top of the boys' division, his next fight would come against the men, and that would pit him directly against two of the greatest athletes of all time. A league that contained Euthymus, his fellow citizen, and Theogenes of Thasos would not be one in which Hagesidamus could anticipate success.

If there is one theme that runs throughout these great games it is, oddly, the avoidance of head-to-head competition between major players. Theogenes and Euthymus did not have a rematch of the finals of 480, Gelon and Hieron both won victories, and the Eleans declined the advice of Themistocles to vandalize Hieron's property. As a result both Gelon and Hieron held banquets to commemorate their success, as well as events where the poetry of Bacchylides and Pindar could receive first performance. Theogenes went somewhat further. Although we know he was exceptionally rich – how else could he pay a fine amounting to a talent, enough money to man a major warship for a month? – we do not know whether he ever commissioned a poem in his own honour. What we do know is that in the aftermath of these games, his wife gave birth to a son whom he named Disolympios or 'Double Olympic', with 'victor' understood.[5]

6

The Olympic Games of 476 BC

The papyrus from Oxyrhynchus that gave us some of our evidence for the games of 480 also offers a list, some of it by now familiar, of the victors for 476:

[Sca]mander the Mitylenian won the *stadion*
[Da]ndis the Ar[g]i[v]e won the *diaulos*
[name lost] the Spartan won the *dolichos*
[name lost] the Tarentine won the pentathlon
[name lost] [the Mar]onite won the wrestling
[Euthymus the Lo]crian from Italy won the boxing
[Theogenes the Th]asian won the pancration
[name lost] [the S]partan won the boys' sprint
[Theognetus the Aegin]etan won the boys' wrestling
[Hag]esi[da]mus the Locrian from Italy won the boys' boxing
[. . .]rus the Syracusan won the *hoplitodromos*
[Ther]on of Agrigentum won the *tethrippon*
Hie[ron] of Syracuse won the horse race. (*Oxyrhynchus Papyrus* n. 222)[1]

But how, in the face of the issues that we have seen dogging these events, did this list finally come into being? How did the Olympics in this age actually work? To get at the answer to these questions we must again depend upon the alliance between text and spade, for the excavations that have been carried out at Olympia have enabled us to learn something of the way the site developed, and to place the critical textual evidence in a physical context.

The modern visitor to Olympia will find the site filled with the remains of ancient buildings, the vast majority of them much later than 476. The great gymnasia that are now visible were all prod-ucts of the fourth century BC, as was the vaulted entrance to the stadium and the formal starting line for foot races that have come to light there. At the time when Theogenes and Euthymus plied their trade, the site contained the stadium, a flat area contained within the oblong bank decorated with war memorials where Gelon left his trophy. Close by the stadium was the equestrian race-track. To the west of these grounds were the temple of Zeus, a temple to his consort Hera, a gigantic altar and a shrine to Pelops. To the northeast of the temple was a row of 'treasuries' built by various cities to show off dedications to the gods, and to the southeast was an administrative building.[2]

Nearly a year before the opening of the games, two men would be appointed as *Hellenodikai*, 'judges of the Greeks', to administer the Olympic festival.[3] They would take up residence in a special house – the Hellenodikeion – and would be charged with over-seeing all aspects of the event (it may also have been the case, early on, that a third person was appointed to instruct them in their duties). Pausanias, who provides this information, says that the two men were 'chosen by lot from amongst all the Eleans'. It is possible that the thinking here was that the lot would fall to those whom the gods supposed would do a good job – which all sounds very good, but the Greeks of the early sixth century BC (Pausanias notes that the office was instituted in 580) were aware that not all men possessed equal levels of competence. It is unfortunate that

Pausanias does not tell us whether there was some mechanism to ensure that 'all the Eleans' did not include those who were noted for their personal ineptitude.

The job of the *Hellenodikai* was anything but a sinecure. It fell to them to make sure that the site – the sanctuary of Zeus was nearly forty miles away from the city – was in good shape; to take charge of the announcing of the games; to ensure that the facilities in Elis itself were sufficient to accommodate the prospective contestants; and finally, they would have both to decide who would be allowed to compete and in what order they would do so. Although certain events were set for specific days of the festival, the actual order in which events took place seems to have been a matter that could be decided on the day.[4]

The job of announcing the games fell to six *theoroi* (sing. *theoros*) – 'ambassadors connected with viewing something connected with the gods' – who were each allotted a part of the Greek world to which they would announce that contestants were invited to the games taking place at the sanctuary of Zeus at Olympia at the time of the full moon in August (or, as it would have been calculated, the second full moon after the summer solstice). These *theoroi* were to proclaim a truce throughout Greece for the month leading up to the games, when all the competitors were supposed to gather at Elis, to train for their events.[5] In each city they would be received by official '*theoros* receivers', who most likely came from families with long-standing connections with the games. In the Greek world of the fifth century BC, where there were no such things as professional diplomats, consular offices or resident ambassadors, diplomacy depended on this sort of personal connection. The official month's truce appears not to have been intended to end wars throughout the world – that would have been impractical – but rather to guarantee safe passage through potentially hostile territory for those who were planning to compete. The games were, after all, in honour of Zeus, and those who competed were on the god's business. It is precisely this aspect of the games that explains why, when Chiot ships were preparing to sink Athenian ships off the coast of Euboea in 480, and Xerxes himself was in the region of Thasos, Xenopeithes and Theogenes were permitted to compete at Olympia.

Athletes would begin to show up at Olympia towards the end of July. Most, if not all, would presumably have come straight there after the Isthmian games, which would serve the same function of gathering people together at a convenient location for the Pythian games in years when the Olympics were not being held. This also meant that an athlete who was planning to compete at Olympia would probably have competed at Isthmia as well, and would have been equipped to stay in the area of the games from late spring (the Isthmian games took place in April–May). The Isthmian games, although attracting far fewer spectators than the Olympics, contained all the elements of the greater festival and, additionally (as befitted a festival where people might warm up for the Pythian games), musical competitions.[6]

For the Isthmian games of 476 we know that Theogenes was definitely there because he won both the boxing and the pancration. It is likely that Dandis of Argos, the victor in the Olympic *diaulos*, was there as well. The fact that Dandis' career lasted twelve years suggests that for all his ability, there was at least one Olympic defeat, and several at Isthmia. The boys' victor in wrestling, Theognetus of Aegina, is known from a Pindaric ode celebrating the victory of his nephew at the Isthmian games many years later.[7] Did Theognetus fail to finish first a few months earlier? The Isthmian games may have been a warm-up for the more prestigious games at Olympia. Losers could have been inspired, victors could have become over-confident, and some people could simply have emerged as irritants. Theogenes of Thasos appears to have fallen very easily into this category.

Once the *theoroi* were sent out it is likely that the *Hellenodikai* had to get to work preparing the site of the games. Greeks of this age were not prone to waste potentially useful agricultural land in the years when there was no good alternative use for it, and were certainly not about to maintain stadia for years of non-use. A text found inscribed on marble from Delphi gives us some impression of what was involved. Items include expenditure for cleaning out the stadium, restoring the seating, levelling the jumping pits for the pentathlon, constructing turning posts; cleaning the hippodrome, fixing the turning posts in the hippodrome, fencing the competition areas (presumably to keep the local wildlife out); acquiring the proper earth for the race-tracks, the right sand for the wrestling pit (which also needed to be dug out at the stadium) and so forth. In the records for the Pythian games of 246 BC there is no one who appears to be a general contractor – each one of these tasks was awarded separately by the officials in charge. The fact that the grounds at Olympia were around forty miles away from the Hellenodikeion at Elis must also have ensured that the *Hellenodikai* spent much of their time on the road, making sure that things actually got done in advance of the opening ceremonies.[8]

Was it easier to deal with the contractors than with the athletes, once they started to arrive? That it should be so might astonish anyone who has done any sort of home renovation, but there seems to have been a basic assumption that the athletes who poured into Elis for the mandatory one-month training period were likely to be rather a pain in the neck. Athletes had to swear on arrival that they had been in training for the previous ten months (how one checked on this we do not know), and, as already mentioned, they had to offer proof that they were citizens of Greek states. The *Hellenodikai* of 476 would, furthermore, have had to deal with the public relations nightmare of Themistocles' attack on Hieron before the games began. The Eleans, truth be told, had not exactly played a stellar role in the repulse of the Persian invasion, and the somewhat predictable response of the city council (which would have advised the *Hellenodikai* at this point) may have contributed to Themistocles' campaign to overthrow the existing regime and replace it with one more 'democratic' and more likely to be aligned with his own increasingly anti-Spartan view of Greece's future.[9]

Not all the issues that came before the *Hellenodikai* were as politically fraught as the admission of the Sicilian tyrants. A fragment of a decree about behaviour at Olympia from some point in the late sixth century BC was discovered in 1964–5 on two broken bronze tablets, once part of a larger text that was evidently nailed to some sort of wooden object. The content of this text seems to have been a list of infractions, in and outside the stadium:

The wrestler will neither break any finger . . .
The arbitrator will [pu]nish by striking except on the head . . .
Those who are polluted are to be rounded up and noted . . .
And [. . .]n the Olympics and he will be judged worthy of victory
  again . . .
Neither a man of the Eleans, an ally or a woman; if knowingly he should
  do wrong
He is not to support a man of Elis or the allies . . .
He should pay [?] drachmas, if he does injury or det[. . .]
Are to be given; with another's money nor a *theoros* . . .
Wars. (Minon *Les inscriptions Éléennes* n. 5)[10]

The first line indicates that offences taking place during a match are included here – where else would a wrestler be breaking a person's finger? – while the reference to the arbitrator's ability to punish harshly anywhere except on the head has been clarified by a text first published in 2007. This text offers a collection of rulings on matters of public entertainment by the emperor Hadrian, and at one point he states that entertainers are to be beaten only on the legs. This is simply an extension of the rule that a contestant could not be hit on the head. The desire to exclude people who were 'polluted' may refer simply to those who broke the Olympic oath, which may indicate that the next line refers to people who have made amends for their violation. The next two clauses may also be explicable with the aid of the Hadrianic text (the traditions of ancient sport were notoriously conservative), where it is stated that an athlete who is applying for admission to the games should not have a local person act as his advocate. Such a person could bring undue influence to bear upon those deciding whether he met the criteria for entry. It is a pity that we cannot tell what the problem is with the *theoroi*, but the context would suggest that it might have to do with people who borrowed money that they did not repay, rather than with result-fixing. A further problem with the *theoroi* figures in another decree that appears to have resulted from a scandal when some were found to have polluted the sanctuary at Olympia by having sex there.[11]

7

The Festival Approaches

The month that the athletes spent in Elis preparing for the games
was most likely a time of increasing anticipation and aggravation.
The spectators may have started showing up in significant numbers as the games got closer, but for many the journey was a long
one. A writer in the fourth century BC, Xenophon, pointed out that
he was unwilling to go to the games from Athens because it was a
five- to six-day walk in each direction (making the total trip a
three-week endeavour). A modest traveller would come with only
a single servant. The philosopher Plato is said to have attended the
games on his own and stayed in a tent with some strangers who
did not know who he was. He was so unpretentious that when the
people he had met there visited him at Athens, they asked if they
could meet his famous namesake the philosopher and were aston-
ished when he said, 'But I am myself that man.'[1]

Irritating and time-consuming though the trip might have been,
many people still made it. It appears that the stadium at Olympia
could accommodate twenty-four thousand spectators at this period,
suggesting that something like thirty thousand might have been
present at any one time (including the athletes and assorted hangers-
on). There could be forty-eight entrants to the chariot race, and
probably as many to the horse race and to two events that would

be eliminated by the mid-fifth century – the mule-cart race and the *kalpe*, a race for mares in which the rider would leap off his horse and run alongside it, holding the reins, for the last lap. While we cannot be absolutely certain as to what the 'pit crew' for a chariot looked like, it is not unimaginable that there would have been around ten men for a chariot or mule cart (a driver, perhaps four grooms, a coach and a chariot-repair man, maybe a cook and other personal attendants), and at least three (the jockey, trainer and groom) for each horse. Each of the four running events could accommodate between twenty-two and forty-four contestants, all of whom would have their trainers and servants with them, while the pentathlon and combat events would probably include another fifty-five or so contestants in the men's division. The boys' events would add another sixty to seventy athletes. All told, Elis would have had two to three thousand more mouths to feed in the month before the games, and ten times that number once the games began. To put this crowd in some kind of proportion, Thucydides allows us to estimate that roughly twenty thousand men were engaged in both sides at the battle of Mantinea in 418 BC (he says, the largest land battle of the generation).[2]

There was only so much that the officials at Elis could do, or were willing to do. When it came to food, by the fourth century there was an official dining hall, but one site could scarcely feed such crowds. Many people brought their own food, and the especially prominent would set up quite elaborate tents. The later-fifth-century BC Athenian politician Alcibiades, who entered seven chariots in the games of 416 in an effort (successful, as it turned out) to win, is said to have shown up with considerable support from cities that were then subordinate allies of Athens, for we are told: 'The Ephesians erected a magnificently decorated tent for him; the city of Chios provided him with food for his horses and with great numbers of sacrificial animals; and the people of Lesbos sent him wine and other provisions for the many great entertainments that he offered' (Plutarch *Alcibiades* 14).[3] Powerful men like Gelon and Theron, even if they did not attend themselves, might also have sent large groups to support their racing teams – certainly the tents erected by later Sicilian tyrants were said to have been magnificent. They and Alcibiades, unlike the worried Athenian we met earlier, would have come by sea and, given that they were bringing horses with them, might well have hired special transport ships for the purpose. The crews would have been in the offing, and required feeding, as the festival took place.

In addition to questions of food, there were the further questions of heat, flies and water. The area of Olympia was notorious for its aggressive population of flies – the Eleans would sacrifice to Zeus, 'Averter of Flies', before the games, but without success. The philosopher Thales is said to have died from heat stroke at the games, and the overall conditions were so uncomfortable that at some point an anecdote began to circulate about a man who had threatened an irritating slave with a trip to Olympia, as a worse fate than being sent to work in a mill. The situation was not helped by the fact that, with the exception of the bath house that the Eleans would build for athletes in the course of the fifth century, there was no regular water supply, and no sanitation system. People dug wells, but it would not be until the fourth century that channels were built to divert the stream of the Alpheus river so that it could supply fresh water to the sanctuary. It did not help the hygiene problem that people tended to use the wells as rubbish dumps. Excavation has revealed them to be filled with crockery. It would be only in the second century AD that the richest man in Greece, Herodes Atticus, would build an aqueduct to bring in fresh water.[4] The fact that there were images of Asclepius, the god of healing,

64

and his female counterpart Good Health at the site of the games may be illustrative of the perception that survival might require a dose of divine intervention.

In the month leading up to the games the *Hellenodikai* would spend their time evaluating the talent, for the grounds could accommodate only a certain number of people. The evidence for lanes in the stadium (there were twenty-two of them) gives us our possible number for the contestants, while the complexity of the pentathlon's scoring system suggests that the number of contestants is not likely to have been more than five. All three of the combat events comprised multiple rounds, but it is unlikely that there were more than four of these. As a result of such limitations, while we cannot now know how many men and boys would be excluded to make these totals, we do know that forty-eight seems to have been the optimal number of contestants in the combat sports, and possibly one hundred and ten in the running events (assuming two heats for the *stadion* and *diaulos*, but not for the distance race, the *dolichos*). A much later text states quite clearly that it was in the training period before the games that a pancratiast developed clear hopes of winning (or not, as the case might be), suggesting that people did indeed use the time to decide who might have a chance. This might also explain why the Eleans should have been concerned about people making false declarations of eligibility; that would have been less of a concern if there had not been pressure on the number of places. The other issue was whether a young man could compete in the boys' or men's division – as Pausanias suggests, the chief criterion was not actual age but rather physical maturity.[5]

As the second new moon after the summer solstice approached, preparations were finalized, and four days before the new moon an official procession set out from Elis on the long hike to Olympia.

Included would be all the athletes, their coaches and fans, official representatives from cities that recognized the Olympic truce, the city council of Elis and the long-suffering *Hellenodikai*. Such a procession was not fast-moving and would spend the night at Pieria, a spring about halfway between the two sites. The next day, once they arrived at Olympia the *Hellenodikai* would administer the oath to all participants (athletes, family members and trainers) that they would do nothing to disgrace the games, and another to the contestants in the men's category that they had trained for ten months, while the judges swore they would do their job fairly. The second day included a parade of the contestants, followed by the equestrian events. The third day, the day of the new moon, opened with the sacrifice of a black ram to Pelops (since days began with sunset, this would actually be on what we would consider to be the night of the second day). In the morning there would be yet another parade, followed by the massive sacrifice of a hundred oxen to Zeus. The afternoon was then given over to the boys' events.[6] The morning of the fourth day was the time for the foot races and the pentathlon, and in the afternoon the combat events would take place. At the very end of the day, the race in armour would be run. The fifth day would include a ceremony at which prizes were awarded, followed by victory celebrations. Quite possibly it was on this day that the first of Pindar's odes for young Hagesidamus of Locris was sung.

The prizes offered at the games were famously symbolic. At Olympia the victor received a palm frond at the time of his initial triumph and an olive crown on the final day. At the Pythian games the crown was of laurel – the laurel was sacred to Apollo – while at Nemea and Isthmia it was made from wild celery leaves. Far greater rewards would await the victors when they returned home.

8

Winning

THE EQUESTRIAN EVENTS

The contests at Olympia were immensely demanding, varied in the skills required, and often quite dangerous. The nature of the four equestrian events, for instance, although run on the same course, changed depending on the number of laps required. So too did the running events in the stadium. The three combat events were simply horrific.

The *keles* – the race at which Hieron's Pherenikos performed so well – was perhaps the most straightforward of the equestrian events. It was a sprint over a single lap. Speed was of the essence and legend had it that a good horse did not even need a rider. There was a story told about a horse named Aura, 'Breeze', who threw her young rider and still finished ahead of the pack. Her owner was awarded the prize – one of two that the mare would win; an owner could take pride in such a beast, who would reflect his own excellent taste. So too might an owner like Hieron take pride in the extraordinary record of Pherenikos, winner not just at these Olympics, but also twice at the Pythian games. His career was all the more remarkable in that it lasted at least six years – by the end of that time it might be expected that a horse was past its best years as a sprinter. The *keles* was probably the first event of the day, and that too may have made it possible for Hieron and Theron to avoid getting in each other's way.[1]

We know much less about the other two races in the hippodrome during these years. The *kalpe* was notable, as already mentioned, in that the riders ran alongside the mares they were racing for the final lap. Otherwise it looks as if the event was modelled on a type of chariot race that was evidently popular at Athens in which an armed man leapt from the chariot, also to run the final lap. This event took place at the grand festival, the Panathenaia, which was founded in that city during the sixth century. If the *kalpe* looked to Athens for inspiration (though this may be more than we can really know), it appears that the inspiration for the mule-cart race, the *apene*, was Sicilian. We can sense the puzzlement that this event, which looks very much like an ancient version of modern harness racing in which a horse pulls a two-wheeled vehicle and its driver, inspired in mainland Greeks. Pindar, for instance, in composing an ode to honour a henchman of Hieron, who may also have been present at the games of 476, suggests that his mules might want to take him on a nice trip to Sparta (they will know the way because they won at Olympia). For Pindar, it would seem, not even a championship turn could relieve him of the impression that he was talking about beasts of burden. Another author of a victory ode suggests that the victor Psaumis of Camerina should delight in the horses of Poseidon. Simonides, in commemorating another winner, described the mules as the 'daughters of swift-footed horses'. In 444, the Eleans would abolish the competition as undignified. This point, made for us by Pausanias, is important as an indication of the way that people thought about events.[2] If one was going to alter a race for being too time-consuming, it would have been the four-horse chariot race, the *tethrippon*.

Our ability to reconstruct the *tethrippon* depends on information of varying types. Pindar, for instance, twice refers to the race as *duodekadromos*, which means 'twelve *dromoi*'. The meaning of *dromos* (singular) here is not immediately obvious, for the word has many meanings in Greece ranging from 'rapid movement', 'somewhat faster movement than usual' (its meaning when Herodotus describes the advance of the Athenian army at Marathon), 'the distance a person could run in a day', to 'race course', 'lane on a race-track' and so forth. With Pindar's usage, the issue is whether *dromos* denotes a length or a lap, and hence whether the race was roughly 3,600 or 7,200 metres.

The difficulty of interpretation is underscored by an ancient commentator who says that 'the men who run the *dolichos* run seven *dromoi* on the course [*dromos*], three going out, three coming back and they finish the seventh at the turning post'. This same commentator adds: 'the chariots round the turning posts [the plural here is important] twelve times'. One early commentator on Pindar offers the explanation that 'ancient chariots did not run seven laps, but rather twelve'; this individual was presumably writing after the last Olympic games in the early fifth century AD, and comparing the race to contemporary races in cities like Constantinople. Another, who seems better informed, says, 'the horse-drawn chariots ran twelve laps, that is twenty-two turning posts'. There are twenty-two turning posts because there are no posts to be turned on the first and last legs of the race, and the precision on this point suggests that this person may have seen such a race. As for its length, the sole piece of ancient evidence, contained on a page of a manuscript from Constantinople, states:

> The Olympic contest has a racetrack of eight *stades*, and, of this, one part is three *stades* and one *plethron*, while the flat before the starting

point is one *stade*, 4 *plethra* for a total of 4800 'feet'. The horses begin to turn around the turning posts in the vicinity of the hero-shrine called the Taraxippus, while the end of the track is near the statue of Hippodameia. Amongst the race horses, the young race horses run six *stades*, the older race horses run 12 *stades*, the younger two-horse chariots run three laps, the older ones run eight laps, the younger four-horse chariots run eight laps, the older run 12 laps.[3]

The figures here include a series of races introduced during the fourth century BC which obviously included a division of horses into older and younger, as well as a two-horse chariot race. The prime event, however, remained the twelve-lap *tethrippon*. A twelve-lap race that covered around seven kilometres (about four miles) along a course that had but two turning posts and no central barrier was inherently dangerous. In fact, danger seems to have been part of the attraction since at the western end of the track there was an altar to Taraxippus, or 'Horse Frightener', while at the other end was a statue of Hippodameia who had (according to some versions of the story) betrayed Oenomaeus to Pelops. The race-tracks at Isthmia and Nemea also had shrines to catastrophe. At Nemea it was a red rock near the far turn of the track, at Isthmia a shrine to a mythological character named Glaucus, who had died in an accident during a chariot race.

The audiences arriving at the hippodrome expected to see the toys of the rich and famous crash into each other, and the length of the race might seem to have been intended not only to ensure that this would happen but also, perhaps, to level the playing field: the victory would go not simply to the person who had the best horses, but also to the person whose charioteer was both extremely skilful and extremely lucky. Not even Hieron or Theron could guarantee that they would be able to satisfy all these conditions in advance. We are told that in one race at Delphi only one of forty-two chariots that started the race actually finished.[4]

Imminent disaster hangs over much of what we hear from the fans of ancient chariot-racing. It is precisely the possibility of self-inflicted failure that the hero Nestor is made to stress in advice that he gives his son Antilochus before the race in the twenty-third book of the *Iliad*:

Antilochus, although you are young, Zeus and Poseidon have taught you all the arts of good horsemanship, and so I do not need to teach you, since you know well how to round the turning post. But your horses are the slowest to run the race, so I think this will be hard for you since [your opponents'] horses are faster, but they do not know better than you how to devise a plan. But come now, dear boy, cast this plan entirely into your heart so that the prizes will not slip past your grasp . . . The one man, confident in his chariot and his horses, thoughtlessly wheels wide on this side and that, his horses drift wide upon the course, and he cannot restrain them; but he who knows cunning arts, although driving slower horses, always watching the turning post, drives close to it, nor does he forget how, from the start, to keep his horses taut to the oxhide reins, and, holding them steady, keeps his eyes on the driver in front . . . You, nearing [the turning post], will drive your chariot and horses close by, and you yourself in your well-woven chariot will lean to your left, and then, calling out, goad your right-hand horse, shaking the reins in your hand; your left-hand horse must shave by the marker so that the hub of the wheel will seem to graze the edge, but do not touch the stone lest you bring the horses to grief and wreck your chariot. That would be joy to others and a matter for shame to yourself. But, dear boy, be smart and be safe, for if in rounding the marker you should slip ahead, there is no one who will catch you, or, sprinting in pursuit, pass you, not even if the man behind you were driving great Arion, swift horse of Adrastus, who was born from the immortals, or Laomedon's horse, who are the pride of those raised here. (*Iliad* 23.306–48)

It was for an audience that had no doubt seen a great deal of this sort of thing that the great playwright Sophocles included a minutely detailed description of crashes at a chariot race at Delphi:

They took their places where the appointed judges had drawn the lots and placed the chariots; at the sound of the bronze trumpet they dashed off, shouting at their horses at the same time they gripped the reins with their hands; the whole track sounded with the clash of rattling chariots . . . They had all been standing upright in their chariots, but then the hard-mouthed colts of the man from Aenia took him off by force, making the turn as they finished the sixth and began the seventh lap and smashed their heads into the chariot from Barce, and then one driver after another broke down and crashed in one great catastrophe, and the whole plain of Crisa was filled with the equestrian shipwreck. Seeing this, the clever charioteer from Athens pulled his horses away and held back, staying away from the confused mass of chariots in the middle of the track. Orestes was the last, keeping his horses back, having faith in the final result, so when he saw the lone driver left he shouted a sharp command at the ears of his swift horses and went in pursuit. They drove level, with the head now of one, now of the other, standing out from the chariots, and he remained straight in his car throughout all the remaining laps, then, as the horse turned he loosened the reins on the left, and unaware he struck the end of the pillar, he shattered the axle box, slid over the rail and, caught in the reins, he fell to the ground as the horses scattered across the middle of the course. (*Electra* 709–48)

Although Nestor's advice on how to win a chariot race would have been good in any era, it is plain that the equestrian events at Olympia had all departed a very long way from the Homeric norm, and they did so in a manner as to make the Sophoclean ending of the race ever more likely. For Sophocles, things start to go very wrong in the middle of the race at the far turning post. In a race so long that the rider was bound to lose control of his team, he was well advised to hang back and let catastrophe overtake his rivals. Even if confident of victory, at the exhausting end of a long course he needed to keep his head, remain cautious and make sure that he made the final turn. How many, even among the most experienced drivers, were dragged to their deaths? And there was no central barrier to prevent head-on collisions, which exacerbated the situation.

THE PENTATHLON AND THE FOOT RACES

The first of the events to be held in the stadium was the pentathlon, and it was immensely challenging, requiring that the champion perform more than decently in at least three skills, all of which differed significantly from each other. So how would a potential winner plan his strategy? This is not an easy question to answer – the way the pentathlon was scored and won has long puzzled modern scholars. In simplest terms, the problem arises from three things that we actually know about this event. The first is that there were five contests held in the following order: *stadion*, discus, long jump (*halma*), javelin and wrestling. The second is that we are told the winner of three contests was the victor; the third, that the last event, wrestling, required that in the end there could be only two finalists. A final complexity, at least as far as the Olympics are concerned, is that the first four events were held in the stadium, while the wrestling was held in front of the great altar of Zeus; and our source for this information makes it clear that not all made it to this stage (referring simply to 'those who made it through to the wrestling').

The rules for a pentathlon that have been preserved on a badly damaged inscription from Rhodes suggest that each contestant would have thrown the discus five times, while Pausanias says that only three discuses were used. Then, in a mythic explanation of the pentathlon, we are told that the first victor – Peleus, father of Achilles – won even though he was victorious only in the wrestling.[5] It is not entirely clear what to make of all this, but it seems probable that the first two events involved the large-scale elimination of contestants, that only first- and second-place winners in the first two events could continue to the third round, and then anyone who was not able to win the three victories (for instance, one of the second-place winners who did not win the long jump) would be eliminated, as would the third-place finisher in the next event, the javelin. This system presumes that if someone manages three victories in the first four events, the pentathlon ends, but also that the final victor may in fact have won only twice; it is perhaps significant that we are not told that you cannot be the winner if you do not win three times, only that you do win if you win three times.

The *stadion* race was a simple sprint of roughly two hundred metres and the victor would have to run two heats on the same day, but it was an event that was plainly intended to highlight a single skill, running very fast. The *diaulos* was a race around the turning post that served as the end line in the *stadion* race and back to the starting line, so also a sprint from beginning to end, and we hear of a number of people who managed to win both in the same Olympiad – from 488 to 480, the astonishing Astylus of Croton in southern Italy (later Syracuse) won both the *stadion* and the *diaulos* in each Olympiad, adding the *hoplitodromos*, the race in armour, in 480.[6] It would be a long time before any comparable athlete would appear on the scene.

The *dolichos* which, as we have seen, was a seven-length race at Olympia, called for very different skills from the two sprints, and only one man was ever able to win all three (something that no modern athlete would even attempt). Elsewhere the *dolichos* was a much longer event, with distances ranging from twelve to twenty-four lengths. In addition to the variation in the number of lengths, there was some variation in what constituted a 'length'. A length, or *stade*, was technically equivalent to six hundred human feet. At Olympia, where the foot used for the measurement was 0.3205 metres, the track was 192 metres; at Delphi, where a shorter foot was used (0.2965 metres), the *stade* was 178 metres. Although this might not seem too great a difference (and in this world without stopwatches no one would try to compare times), it is impossible to imagine that it would not have had an impact on runners who hoped to use a final kick-sprint to carry the day. Some champions at Olympia might simply have run out of space to catch an opponent in a sprint on a shorter track.[7]

The *hoplitodromos* stands out from the other events in that, while the last three are all straightforward contests of athletic ability, this race is an endurance contest. At places other than Olympia, where it was required that the contenders all carry torches along with their pieces of armour, it seems to be the sort of event that was dreamed up by fans who wanted to see their athletes performing well outside their comfort zone. Like the *kalpe* it resembles something of a theatrical performance; like the *tethrippon* it also had the appearance of an event where people might well crash into each other. It also varied immensely in length from place to place. The Olympic race in armour was a two-lap race like the *diaulos*, the version run at Nemea was four lengths, while at games that were instituted at Plataea to commemorate the final victory over the Persians, it was fifteen lengths. At the inception of the race the runners were required to wear a helmet, carry a shield and wear greaves on their legs. In 450 BC the rules would be changed so that the greaves were removed. Otherwise, as with all other events held in the stadium, the runner was naked.

The inconsistency in the lengths of the *dolichos* and the *hoplitodromos*, as well as the change in equipment of the latter just mentioned, raises questions about the forces that influenced the development of events at the games. On the one hand, the great length of the *hoplitodromos* at Plataea might have been determined by the length of the final charge of the Spartans against the Persians that won the day; but the adoption of the sport cannot be explained by any single factor – any more than can the fact that the athletes in the stadium were all nude. It also seems clear that, despite the effort to provide lanes, a runner was reasonably advised to try to take the lead fast and avoid the elbows of his fellow competitors, or being tripped. Depictions of runners stress their powerful legs and upper bodies.[8] These are especially visible, of course, because the athletes have nothing on.

NUDITY

The Greeks themselves attributed athletic nudity to the fact that a sprinter named Orsippus lost his loincloth while winning the *stadion* race at Olympia in 720 (or Olympiad 15, according to Hippias of Elis), and was so inspired by the event that he afterwards ran without one.[9] In fact, the adoption of nudity in athletics was plainly something that took place over a number of years in the course of the sixth century BC. The evidence for this change comes from the representation of Greek athletes on works of art (in all cases, painted pottery), where we can see the shift from athletes who are loinclothed in the Homeric fashion, to nude in the new style.

Stories about Orsippus existed already by the time that Hippias came to compile his list. So much may be gleaned from the fact that there was a statue of the proto-nudist celebrating his glory in the market-place of Megara, where there was also a shrine to the hero Coroebus, who might be the same Coroebus who was the first winner of the *stadion* race and was also celebrated at a shrine on the border of Elis. Thucydides, however, attributed the origin of naked competition to the Spartans and stated that the change took place in the not too distant past.[10] In doing so he may again have been implicitly denying something that Hippias asserted. In any event, the traditions about Coroebus serve as a reminder that, despite great interest in the topic, there could be no 'official' history of sport (or of anything else) in the Greek world.

The origins of athletic nudity may, in fact, have little to do with sport and a great deal to do with ideas about status. It was in the eighth century BC that the artistic convention of depicting Greek males unclothed developed. To be naked, it seems, was to be worth seeing; it was a costume rather than an assertion of sexuality or an invitation to eroticism per se (though it did not exclude either). By the sixth century, being naked might reveal a man to be Greek rather than barbarian. Herodotus says that the Lydian neighbours of the Greeks were ashamed to be seen naked, and has the Persians marvel at the three hundred naked Spartans exercising before the battle of Thermopylae in 480. Thucydides, too, notes that the choice to exercise without clothing distinguishes the Greek from the barbarian. More than that, however, to be naked was also to be young, to be capable, not to be 'past it', to be Greek and strong; and perhaps that is all, originally, that mattered.

Nudity cannot, therefore, be associated with ancient sporting custom – Homer's athletes wear loincloths, as do athletes depicted in the Bronze Age. And it would seem to have nothing obvious to do with the worship of the gods whose acolytes kept their clothes on at all times – and avoided having sex, which does not seem to have been a particularly common trait amongst Greek athletes, one of whom is reported as having boasted that after a morning in the nude on the wrestling ground, there was nothing like an afternoon with his boyfriend in bed. Indeed, if there was no sense of an erotic component to watching well-conditioned men, all rubbed down with olive oil before they showed themselves to their fans, then it would be hard to understand why women, who could be present in the *Odyssey*, could not be present at Panhellenic games while men were competing. The fact that fans liked the 'uniform' that athletes adopted in the course of the sixth century may have played some role in the institutionalization of the practice of athletic nudity. In the fourth century BC, Aristotle would assert that nature wished to distinguish the bodies of free men from slaves, making those of the former 'straight and unsuited for such labours' as those performed by slaves. In putting things as he does, he quite likely summarizes the ideology behind athletic nudity – looking good in the buff was a sign that one possessed what it took to be a contender.[11] It also marked the athlete as someone special and, to survive the events in which he competed, special was what he needed to be.

PAIN AND SUFFERING

Nudity is one thing, the implication of competing in armour another, and one may wonder whether the latter should be taken to imply a connection between sport and training for war. The answer to this question hinges on the definition of terms – if one means by this 'training for combat' the answer is likely no, but if it means an 'interest in military drill', the answer may be quite different. A foot race in partial equipment was not per se a military activity any more than was the *kalpe*. The fact that greaves were later eliminated from the *hoplitodromos* outfit would, further, imply that the athletes themselves protested – it is obvious that someone must have complained, or there would have been no reason to change something that had been the practice for seventy years. Both the *kalpe* and the *hoplitodromos* do, however, suggest that people liked to watch demonstrations of physical skill by people bearing arms; the fact that the race came to be the last one at a festival may mean that, once established, it assumed a new significance. By the third century AD it was possible to state:

> [The *hoplitodromos*] was given a place in the contests to signify the
> resumption of the state of war, the shield indicating that the truce of
> God is past and one has need of weapons. If one listens attentively
> to the herald, one perceives that he is announcing to the assembled
> people that the contest for prizes is at an end. (Philostratus *Concerning
> Gymnastics* 7, tr. Woody)

By the time these words were written, there was no chance of anyone taking up arms against a neighbour (they were all then ruled by the Romans), but since Philostratus says that his view is based upon what the herald said, his statement about the symbolic placement of the event is plausible.

The race in armour, like the *kalpe*, was taken up to please the fans, and it was through dialogue with the fans that these events were shaped and given new meaning. Later, once the *kalpe* and the *synôris* (a race with a chariot drawn by two horses) were eliminated, new equestrian events would be added to bring in mares and younger horses. It is not unreasonable to imagine that these events were added to the Olympic programme because, with but two races left, the day allotted for equestrian displays had become insufficiently full.

The interests of the fans may also be at work in the development of events that were held just before the *hoplitodromos*, on the last afternoon of competition. These were the wrestling, boxing and pancration. Boxing and wrestling, both of which were known to Homer as 'painful', were widespread in the ancient world, but pancration was a peculiarly Greek sport, combining boxing and wrestling in a unique – and uniquely violent – way.

On the day of the contest, the ordinary practice was to hold the wrestling first, boxing second and the pancration third. This order was, however, at the discretion of the *Hellenodikai*, who could change it if they thought there was a good reason to do so. By the time the games were held in 476, there are no grounds for thinking that they had been given such a reason, and the rebarbative conduct of Theogenes in 480 was a decided inducement not to do so. Many years later, however, when both a boxer and a wrestler wished to compete in the pancration in addition to their own sports, the situation had changed. The following story is known to us through Pausanias:

At the Isthmian Games Clitomachus won the men's wrestling-match, and on the same day he defeated all competitors in the boxing-match and in the pancration. His victories at the Pythian Games were all in the pancration, three in number. At Olympia, Clitomachus was the first after Theagenes of Thasos to be proclaimed victor in both boxing and the pancration. He won his victory in the pancration at the hundred and forty-first Olympic Festival [216 BC]. The next Festival saw this Clitomachus a competitor in the pancration and in boxing, while Caprus of Elis intended both to wrestle and to compete in the pancration on the same day. After Caprus had won in the wrestling-match, Clitomachus put it to the Hellenodikai that it would be fair if they were to bring in the pancration before he received wounds in the boxing. His request seemed reasonable, and so the pancration was brought in. Although Clitomachus was defeated by Caprus he tackled the boxers with sturdy spirit and unwearied vigour. (*Description of Greece* 6.15.3–5, Loeb tr., slightly adapted)

So that these events might be run efficiently, it was extremely important that an even number of contestants entered them. A bye was a tremendous advantage, given the pounding that people would endure (hence Theogenes missed the pancration in 480), and it was entirely likely that in the course of a contest at least one winner would be unable to advance, providing a prospective opponent in the next round with a break. That this was a major issue can be gleaned from the boast of a pancratiast in the early second century AD that he fought his opponent in the finals so hard that the Eleans declared a draw, to the honour of both – but that, unlike his opponent, he had had no respite. Although hundreds of years separate these events, continuity in the way the sport was organized created specific, and predictable, circumstances – circumstances that the fans would have anticipated as they took their seats.[12]

The wrestling, boxing and pancration had to be completed in time for the *hoplitodromos* to be run before the sun went down, so it is likely that they began as soon as possible once the running events were over. With sunrise in Greece coming around 6.30 in the morning during August (and sunset around 8.30), there would be just enough time to complete all the action. We are told that the officials ended one second-century AD pancration match in a draw because the stars of evening were appearing in the sky, meaning that the match had to be stopped if the final race was to be held.[13]

The running events may not have taken more than a few hours to complete, but on any reckoning the time allotted to the combat events must have been extraordinarily compressed in comparison to the modern descendants of these three sports – that is to say, Olympic-style wrestling (but not what we now call Greco-Roman wrestling, which excludes the ground wrestling that was an important aspect of the ancient sport), boxing and, now, the Ultimate Fighting Championship (a most inferior form of pancration).

In no ancient sport was there a time limit or rounds, and each match had to come to a definite conclusion, which in the case of wrestling might have been especially difficult in that the winner had to score three falls against his opponent. So, too, the boxer would need to beat his opponent into submission, since there could be no victory 'on points'. Given that there would be rounds before the finals for each of these sports in the men's division, and that all matches were held in succession, forty-five matches would have to be fought to a conclusion within, perhaps, ten hours.[14] These numbers imply that the expected length of a match was about ten minutes (allowing time to get people into and out of the ring). To win a championship a contestant in the 'heavy events', as they were called, had to contend for around forty minutes over a three-hour span against first-rate opposition. The challenge of contesting multiple rounds in quick succession would seem to have had a significant impact on the conduct of a match. For men like Clitomachus and Caprus this meant eight contests within six hours, and one may well imagine what Caprus thought when Clitomachus convinced the judges to have him take part in the pancration just after winning his four matches. That he could win eight consecutive matches marks him as one of the truly great Olympic champions of all time.

Ancient wrestling differed from modern Olympic wrestling in four important ways (aside from the absence of a clock). The first is that the match did not take place on a mat, but in a specially prepared ground that had been dug out of the stadium and filled with softer sand; the second, that there were no weight classes; the third, that there was no possibility of winning on points; and the fourth difference is in the definition of a fall. A fall in modern wrestling is defined simply as pinning an opponent's shoulders to the mat. The situation is less clear in antiquity, but it seems that a fall was defined as laying out an opponent on either his face or his back. It might also have been possible to force a concession by strangling him, or, in the case of one notorious individual of the mid-fifth century BC, breaking his fingers. The fact that this move had been plainly declared illegal by the end of the sixth century appears to have been forgotten.

In general terms, the pressure for quick victories meant that wrestlers might prefer spectacular moves. The body slam (lifting the opponent off the ground and smashing him on to the sand) was one of those moves – and hence one frequently illustrated in art – and potentially useful in that the individual slammed might not be able to continue. The same could be true of a man caught in an arm lock and twisted on to his back (some versions of these moves which involve pressuring an arm at more than 90 degrees, as represented in ancient art, are classified as illegal in the Fédération Internationale des Luttes Associées and National Collegiate Athletic Association rule books). To be in a position to use moves like this, a wrestler had to be in complete control of his rival. To judge from many depictions in art, a typical attack began with some sort of standing dive for a leg, or other move so as to slip behind the other wrestler and from there to strengthen the advantage. An ancient wrestling manual describes a number of trips and shoulder throws suggesting that, in modern terms, the Olympic champion would be especially good at a take-down. The conditions of matches are further reflected in inscriptions honouring victors who are described as having won 'without suffering a fall' or 'without having been grasped about the waist'.[15]

Perhaps the most famous match in Olympic history, however, was decided not by body slams, arm locks or leg dives so much as by their avoidance. This match was the one in which a young wrestler from the city of Croton in southern Italy defeated a compatriot, who was arguably the greatest wrestler in the history of ancient sport. Milo of Croton, the man defeated, had won six previous Olympic titles and six Pythian ones. Milo's style seems to have been based upon his enormous strength and ability to body-slam his opponents. Timasitheus, who must have known Milo's style well, won by staying out of his grasp until he collapsed of exhaustion.[16]

Boxers, like wrestlers, aimed to gain as rapid an advantage as possible – fighting without weight classes, point systems or rounds, they needed to disable their rival in order to advance. We do not know the size of the ring in which they fought, but it seems that it would have been laid out in the centre of the stadium and was small enough that the referee had to work to ensure both fighters stayed within it. The preferred way of reaching a swift conclusion was through blows to the head, aiming for a knock-out or to force surrender, signified by the beaten man's raising a finger in the direction of the match referee, who was supposed to keep things going by making sure that the boxers did not clinch. We cannot know if the shin-kicking recommended as an important tactic in the third century AD was a significant part of the sport at this point.[17]

Victorious boxers expected to be battered; the sight of one whose face did not display signs of damage was unusual, and a boxer whose defensive technique was so good that one could say that no one landed a punch on him was rare indeed. Illustrations of boxing do, at times, show blood flying.[18] Hands alone were protected, with leather thongs designed to support the wrist and cushion the knuckles.

The most obvious boxing injuries would have been loss of teeth and broken noses. The most serious injuries were less obvious. Knock-out punches in boxing stem from concussions.[19] Not all concussions are equally severe, but repeated traumatic injury leaves the victim ever more susceptible to some life-threatening event; it is this that makes the long careers of Euthymus and Theogenes so remarkable, for they must have been able to overwhelm opponents without suffering many serious injuries to themselves.

Blows that were not to the head were perhaps as likely to be aimed at the genitals, as shown in graphic detail on a sixth-century vase now in the Rome's Villa Giulia Museum. We do not, of course, know whether that blow would have excited the admiration of the crowd, but the stress on blows to the head elsewhere suggests that it might not have. So, too, the story of an odious man named Damoxenus suggests that 'real men' in the boxing ring aimed to hit each other in the head. In Damoxenus' case, the sun was setting in a championship match and the judges asked that he and his rival, Creugas, decide the match by allowing the other a single blow. After Damoxenus survived the one to his head he told Creugas to protect his face, then struck him under the rib cage, allegedly penetrating his body so as to seize his entrails; this would, in fact, have been feasible if Damoxenus had developed a technique similar to the 'spear-hand thrust' known in modern tae kwon-do, and aimed for the spleen. Creugas died, but the judges disqualified Damoxenus.[20]

Pancration, the third of the combat sports, is first attested on an inscription of the mid-sixth century. It combined boxing and wrestling and was contested in the boxing ring rather than on the wrestler's sand. As such it attracted champions in both sports – men like Theogenes and Caprus – as well as its own specialists. It

was the man who could win in both his own sport and the pancration who was considered a true heir to Hercules, and so it was
the men who won in both at the same games who were listed as
his successors. We have entries in victor catalogues to the effect
that 'Caprus the Elean won the wrestling and pancration and was
proclaimed the second after Hercules' (according to ancient methods
of counting, being the 'second after' was the same as the 'first since'),
until the games in 37 AD when the Eleans declared, after proclaiming
Nicostratus of Argos the 'eighth since Hercules', that they would
proclaim no other. More ominously, the entry for 564 BC reads that
Arrachion of Phigelea was crowned although he was dead. The full
version of the story ran that his opponent conceded from the pain
of a suddenly dislocated ankle just before Arrachion expired (he
broke his own neck, executing the move that won the match).[21]
Such an outcome was obviously not ideal, but the even more limited rules that governed this sport – only biting and gouging were
excluded – and the allowance of choke holds, made it a plausible
way for a bout to end. That said, pancration bouts normally did
end in surrender (again signified by a raised finger in the general
direction of an official).

With boxers and wrestlers trying their hand at pancration,
attempting to use their dominance in a particular fighting style to
achieve victory, the sport would seem to have developed as a way
to answer the fan's question: who was the better athlete, the boxer
or the wrestler? Death was a potential result of all combat sports,
and there are stark warnings throughout the evidence from antiquity about the perils of these three forms. To dream that one was
a boxer, for instance, was a very bad thing because it portended
imminent bodily harm.

Even more disturbing is the Athenian legal principle that accidental killing of an opponent in an athletic event amounted to

unintentional homicide. We cannot tell how often this happened, but it is worth noting that in stories such as those of Damoxenus the fact that the judges ruled he could not have the crown seems to be significant. If Damoxenus had not struck a foul blow, he might have been permitted to hold the title – or so we may surmise from the fact that an athlete who killed a man might actually boast about it on an inscription. So, too, a pancratiast who died was described as a victim of 'bad luck'. A medical text attributed to Hippocrates, the father of Greek medicine, tells of a wrestler named Hipposthenes who fell backwards with his opponent on top of him on 'hard ground'. He took a cold bath and awoke the next day with a fever and a dry cough, and his breathing was heavy. Four days later he began to spit up blood, and collapsed into a coma. He died the next day. Camelus of Alexandria, who fought under the name Good Spirit (*Agathos Daimon*), won a boxing title at Nemea at some point in the third century AD and died 'praying to Zeus either for a crown or for death'. Contending for Olympic glory, he may simply have suffered one concussion too many – he was thirty-five.[22]

Deadly, exhausting and dramatic, the games of the Olympics and other festivals were not simple recreations of an epic model. In some cases the rules were very different – multiple laps for chariot races; three out of five falls in wrestling meaning defeat, rather than two out of three; differentiation between types of foot races – and there was constant development. Even if Hippias' list is a fabrication, it does at least show a consciousness of the fact that sport was never frozen in time.

The process of evolution also represents the interests of various groups. Rarely can this be said to be those of the participants – the only thing that we see athletes changing is to do with the wearing of greaves in the *hoplitodromos*. The main chariot race, the *tethrippon*, is much longer, and consequently more dangerous, than its Homeric predecessor, while other events such as the *synoris* and *kelês* (both seemingly Sicilian in origin) seem to have been added to appeal to the interests of people who lived far from Elis. The two 'armed events', the *kalpe* and the *hoplitodromos*, appear to respond to interest in 'drill' rather than actual warfare. Indeed, the fact that there was no descendant of the spear fight in the *Iliad* suggests that people were interested in keeping sport separated, to some degree, from the practice of warfare.

Although the Eleans did little to make the Olympic experience more comfortable for their visitors, they do seem to have tried to make it interesting. They wished to see challenges that were harder on the contestants, and involved potential suffering. The ability to win through great difficulty, to deal with suffering, was an important aspect in Greek thought as we see it emerge during the fifth century, and in this way the games seem to reflect a general move towards sport as an expression not simply of status, but also of character. These characteristics also appear in the way that events were remembered. It is a sign of the importance of sport in the consciousness of Greek society, at the turn of the sixth to fifth century BC, that sport history was being recorded in much more detail than the history of any state.

9

Remembering Victory

Pindar presents himself as the high priest of memory. It was through his words that men and their victories would be immortalized. In fact he faced a great deal of competition in his role as 'panegyrist in chief of the athletic community. As is the case with all self-promotional claims, Pindar's need to be read with considerable scepticism; his work is but part of a commemorative corpus that began to flourish in the last quarter of the sixth century. These acts of individual celebration, which may be seen as an early phase in the development of the sense of the individual as a vital element in human society, are a fundamental contribution of fifth-century Greece to the tradition of Western thought. As would be true in the great plays of Aeschylus, which were beginning to be written even as Pindar sang, or those of Sophocles, athletic commemoration would raise fundamental issues of the place of the extraordinary individual in society. Did he achieve simply for himself, as did the Homeric hero, or rather to bring glory to his community? And how did a community deal with a person whose achievements placed him, to some degree, outside the narrow confines of the life of his own city?

The competitive world of ancient athletic commemoration is also, for us, a somewhat quieter place than it would have been in the ancient world itself – we deal in texts and objects that are lacking what was once a soundtrack and dance routine. The poetry of a Pindar or a Bacchylides was meant to be sung by a chorus, yet we have no score to go with the poems, and we do not even know whether the poet would have provided one himself, or participated in the choreography. Without the music, or even the knowledge of whether there would have been a consistent score to which Pindar's poetry could be sung, we cannot now know if the impression (formed on the basis of his tortured syntax, impossibly varied metres and allusive style) that his work represented the ancient equivalent of gangsta rap is reasonable; or if the more straightforward metres and clearer narrative form (if not always relevant to the issues at hand) that characterize Bacchylides signal that the performance of his work would have been more aligned with that of a modern gospel singer. Nor can we really know how long it would have taken to sing and dance the hundred or so lines of a typical full-blown victory ode.

We do know, however, that the poems were meant to be performed by choruses in public places, and in the victor's hometown. It is likely that these choruses consisted of young men. One of the advantages of praise poetry, in Pindar's view, was that, unlike a statue, it was transferable, making it possible to spread the fame of a victor throughout the world – some of his poetry was probably performed more than once, and in cities other than those in which the victor resided. A sculptor might reply that a statue in the right place was not all that different from a poem: at Olympia, once the habit took root, one could count on thousands of people stopping by every few years to recall an individual's moment of glory. The options of poem or statue were not mutually exclusive, of course, though either required considerable resources. A bronze statue in this period cost about as much as it would take to run one of the standard warships for a month, while the performance of a choral ode (exclusive of whatever fee was paid to the poet) might cost a tenth as much. We have no way of knowing what the poet might have charged in addition to providing the script, but the figures that we have suggest an ancient perception that the sums were significant.[1] It is also the case that both depended on the artist's ability to use existing media of expression – Greek athletes have a tendency, in art, to look very much like other Greek athletes, and Pindaric victors presumably valued the fact that their deeds would be assimilated to myth and remembered with bits of pop philosophy, just as the triumphs of their athletic predecessors had been. Athletics in the Greek world, then, although extended somewhat beyond the restricted circle envisioned in Homer, was anything but a democratic occupation.

The development of both praise poetry – the first famous exponent was a man named Ibycus whose career peaked in the 520s BC – and commemorative statuary is coincidental with the decline in a particular style of government that became increasingly common throughout Greece in the first half of the sixth century, and continued to flourish in areas like Sicily (hence the careers of Hieron and Theron): tyranny.

The successful tyrant was a man who could harness the competitive urges of his fellow aristocrats, and often provide for the welfare of the average citizen. One of the most successful tyrannies in Greece was that of Pisistratus who, along with his sons, dominated Athens for much of the sixth century. Indeed, it was the ejection of Pisistratus' son Hippias in 510 that marked the closure of the last 'tyrannical' regime on the mainland. Well before that time, however, there was evidence to suggest that members of the Athenian aristocracy who felt that Pisistratus overshadowed them had sought to assert the status that was overshadowed at home through victories at the Olympics and elsewhere. There is a dedication to the god Apollo at a shrine in southern Boeotia commemorating chariot victories by a member of an aristocratic household that claimed especial hostility to Pisistratus; and the head of another great clan that raised very good race horses and won the Olympic *tethrippon* found it advisable to become a tyrant in his own right on the Gallipoli peninsula of European Turkey. One of this man's relatives, Cimon, won three successive Olympic championships in the *tethrippon*. The first occurred while he was in exile for opposition to Pisistratus, and after the second he had Pisistratus proclaimed the victor so that he would allow him to come home. Pisistratus' sons murdered him after the third. Pisistratus himself championed a local festival that had been revamped shortly before he came to power as a celebration for all Athenians. The new festival was the Panathenaia, and contained the possible forerunners of the *kalpe* and *hoplitodromos* as well as other 'weapons exercises', musical contests and the naked events that took place at the other festivals. The Panathenaia also offered lavish prizes that the others did not, suggesting that Pisistratus might have been trying to steal some of those competitions' thunder.[2]

Elaborate prizes with an overtly Athenocentric agenda could not, however, displace the existing games with their 'all-Greek' ideals. It was precisely this neutrality that mattered. At Olympia and the other Panhellenic sites, either in verse or statue form, tyrant and rival were on a par. Indeed, ideological homogenization was the order of the day. Pindar's patrons are all people of excellent family (many have a god or hero in their background), skilled through innate ability, ostensibly handsome, honest and brave. Often they have won multiple victories – does the commissioning of an ode sometimes mark the end of a career? – and are the delight of their cities. Losers, we are told, must slink home in shame.

The original dedications at athletic sanctuaries tended towards the tools of victory. The earliest surviving 'victor monuments' are mostly discuses or *halteres*, the weights that long-jumpers used in the pentathlon. These are inscribed with a brief text along the lines of 'Epainetus won at the long jump because of these *halteres*' or 'Echoidas dedicated me to the children of Great Zeus, the bronze with which he defeated the great-hearted Cephallnians.' It was only in the second half of the sixth century that the new style of dedication, involving a statue of the victor, began to supplement the old. The earliest of these would have been carved in stone: naked young men with long hair, the standard style of representation in that era. Around 500 BC stone began to give way to bronze as the primary medium, and increasing realism replaced the stylized figures of the previous era. Realism meant that the men looked more like men, horses more like horses and so forth. There was no true portrait sculpture at this point, and the purpose of the statue was to represent the idea of victory. Hence one victor tends to look like another. As a group they are notable for short-cropped hair, well-toned bodies, designer pubic hair and genital display.[3]

THE ATHLETE AS HERO

Statues at this time and place do not represent the common man, or the ideal of the average. They are intended to reify the ideal of the extraordinary that Pindar also commemorates. But both statues and victory songs considerably understate the role of the great athlete in contemporary imagination. Indeed, even Great King Darius of Persia knew that athletes had to be very special in the world of his Greek subjects, for he gave particular welcome to a doctor from Sicily whose primary claim to fame was that he had married Milo of Croton's daughter.[4]

Fans of men like Theogenes and Euthymus imagined that they had extraordinary qualities. In the intensely demanding physical contest through which these men put themselves, the crucial edge in the quest for victory was as much psychological as physical. Indeed, in modern sport, upset victories will stem as much from the willingness of the underdog to feel he or she has a chance as from the favoured party having a very bad day. Ancient athletes were no strangers to the notion that a good public relations campaign could help. Milo put on displays of strength outside the ring to enhance his reputation. He also wore a lion skin and carried a club, both accessories of Hercules.

Divinities were still widely believed to be active in the Greek countryside during the fifth century BC. The great runner Phidippides, who carried messages back and forth between Athens and Sparta at the time of the Persian invasion of 490, evidently claimed that he had seen the god Pan in the course of his travels. He died bringing news of the victory at Marathon to his fellow citizens – a run of just over twenty-six miles (the only Marathon in the modern sense that was ever run in antiquity). It was during this battle that an Athenian named Epizelus claimed he was blinded by a great hero who had helped turn the battle at a crucial stage. It was generally believed that Apollo had intervened to halt the column that Xerxes sent to wreck Delphi in the course of the campaign of 480, and people said that a divine shout was heard as the battle of Salamis got under way.[5] It might also have come naturally, in a world where athletic victors had their triumphs paired with the deeds of mythic champions by the likes of Pindar and Bacchylides, to tell stories about them evoking thoughts of earlier heroes. Not all these stories would be positive. Great athletes could be difficult people to deal with, and both success and failure could be hard to handle. It is also easy to imagine that a great fighter, habituated to violence through constant training, might fail to control himself. Hercules, after all, was prone to fits of homicidal madness, and many looked to him as a model for their own lives.

The equation between divinities and athletes was well established by the time the games of 476 opened, even if Theogenes hadn't started telling people that Hercules was really his father, and Euthymus might not yet have been spreading the tale that he was the son of the river god Kaikinos. People would have known that the boxer Glaucus of Carystus, who ended his life as a senior official of Hieron's brother Gelon, claimed descent from a sea god. He was a contemporary of Milo. So too might people have known the sad tale of Cleomedes of Astypalaia (an island in the Aegean), who had been refused the Olympic boxing title because he had killed his opponent in a moment of gross brutality. Returning home he had gone mad, destroyed the local schoolhouse (while occupied) and locked himself in a chest that was later found to be empty. Apollo, when consulted on this matter, had said that they should sacrifice to Cleomedes, since he was no longer amongst the mortals.

Apollo had said something similar in the case, now some years in the past, of the pentathlete Euthycles, a man from Euthymus' home city, who had died while imprisoned on a false charge of corruption. The Achaeans might even then have been wondering why they had had no victor in the sprint since the time of Oebates, whose eighth-century victory was, by 476, a long way back in the past. They would finally get around to erecting a statue in his honour during the next decade, at which point an Achaean sprinter was promptly victorious. Milo of Croton did not receive a cult, but people were certainly still talking about him. They might recall the tale that when he was summoned to receive his crown some thirty-four years earlier, when no one dared oppose him, he had slipped.

When the crowd laughed he pointed out that if that was one fall, someone might want to try to chalk up a couple more against him. They might also recall that he had carried his own statue to join the others at Olympia, and invited people to try and force him off a greased discus upon which he would stand.[6]

Although we cannot know whether the presence of one athletic hero in his hometown of Locris sparked the ambitions of Euthymus (or was it simply rivalry with Theogenes?), the fact that such stories concentrate around athletes, and may inspire specific behaviours on their part, is significant. Athletes could be seen as existing, in a curious way, both in the centre of civic societies that valued their achievements and on the fringes of those same societies because their abilities set them apart from other people. A hero in the Greek sense was an ambivalent character, a creature both of awesome power and of considerable menace. Euthymus played upon this when he had inscribed on his statue the words: 'Euthymus of Locris, son of Astycles, having won three times at Olympia, set this up to be admired by mortals.'[7] Some took the last phrase to be obnoxious, intimating that Euthymus was claiming to be more than mortal. Once he was dead and Apollo asserted the point, the text was restored.

In the case of Theogenes, who is said at the age of nine to have carried a bronze statue of a god away from its proper place in the city market-place (and then put it back), it would also be Apollo who would insist on the payment of heroic honours. The story went that a rival showed up at night and flogged the statue of Theogenes which, annoyed at his conduct, fell upon him with predictably fatal results. The man's sons charged the statue with murder and, winning a conviction, had it thrown into the sea. Famine set in, Apollo was consulted and a shrine, part of which still exists, was erected. An inscription, carved a century or so after Theogenes' career ended, tells us:

People who sacrifice to Theogenes are to contribute no less than an obol in the offering box. Anyone who does not make the aforementioned offering will be remembered. The money collected each year is to be given to the high priest, who will save it until it reaches a total of one thousand drachmas. When this total is collected, the council and assembly will decide if it should be spent for some decoration or for repairs to the shrine of Theogenes.

Since there were six obols to a drachma, the Thasians seem to have thought that a lot of people would, over time, be visiting Theogenes' shrine.

Yet another man – this one the recipient of an ode from Pindar for his victory in boxing during the Olympics of 460 – was not only the forefather of a string of Olympic champions, but was so honoured by his city that it inscribed Pindar's ode in gold letters in a local temple. People said that he too was the son of Hermes.[8] The tales of athletes, the celebration of their victories and the grounds upon which they contended were plainly well established by the time Pherenikos raced to victory, or when Theogenes and Euthymus pummelled their opponents into submission in 476, with Pindar proclaiming that the games had been founded by Hercules.

But how did these games come into being?

10

The Emergence of the Panhellenic Cycle

There is no direct line of descent that can take us from the funeral games described by Homer to the events of 476 BC. Individual events such as the *tethrippon* or the wrestling had changed significantly; new sports had emerged, while events that Homer included in the games for Patroclus no longer had a place on the agenda. That said, the games were still almost exclusively the preserve of the very wealthy, people who could afford to travel with substantial entourages for long periods and devote themselves to training at the highest level.

The one exception to this rule seems to have been the *tethrippon*, an event so prestigious that a state might sponsor a team at public expense (as Argos did in 480) to carry away the prize. Unlike at the games in Homer, victory no longer redounded solely to the credit of the winner; it also enhanced the prestige of the city in which he resided. There is no suggestion in Homer, for instance, that the winner in any event went back to his tent and hired someone to produce a song-and-dance routine about his victory in the way that the father of Hagesidamus seems to have done for him. Alcibiades would say, of his time at the Olympics, that he could contend only in the chariot race because in other events he would risk losing to people from 'lesser cities', something that would be unthinkable to a person who fancied himself as much as Alcibiades did.[1]

The most obvious difference between the games as they appear in Homer – both at the death of Patroclus and on Phaeacia – and those at Olympia is that these latter games are linked with cult. The move from private to public in this way is connected with certain trends that are visible in the archaeological record for the development of Greek states in the course of the eighth and seventh centuries BC. Not all places and regions were equally affected by these changes, and not all cities took on identical forms – what we see again is that people are making choices about the way they want their societies to look, rather than adhering to a prescribed plan of development over the years.

The temple was, however, among the most significant new aspects of developing states in Greece.[2] Indeed, well before there were cities, there were sanctuaries, many of them located in areas that would remain on the boundaries of later city-states. These sanctuaries were often the homes of divinities associated with great transitions such as birth or marriage, or with warfare. Some of these shrines rested on the same spots as sanctuaries from earlier ages, or nearby. Certain sanctuaries were established in the context of burials from the age of Mycenaean palaces, while others developed as the communities around them evolved. By occupying neutral ground the shrines could become focal points where people might gather, but these same groups might have other places, often associated with the house of a leading family, in their own settlements where rituals to the gods and communal meals could be held.

The political landscape of Greece began to change as larger political units became visible during the eighth century. The old shrines remained important, but still outside the area of new, much more densely inhabited settlements into which the population of the earlier settlements now moved. The process, which is summed up well by the Greek work *synoikismos* (literally, 'dwelling together'), was gradual, and there are times when it seems that the settlements spreading out of the developing Greek states were more clearly organized than the ones they left behind, possibly as settlers took with them a clear sense of what a city should look like that could best be realized in the absence of earlier structures.

The movement of Greeks abroad is a crucial feature of the development of mainland states. The way was led, it seems, by adventurers from Euboea who established a wide-ranging network of trading settlements stretching from Al Mina in Syria to the island of Pithecoussae in the bay of Naples. The western settlement was established around 770 BC, and it appears that the substance, above all else, that drew the Greeks west was tin. With copper, tin could be forged into bronze, a critical substance in the armouries of the world. As the Greeks moved west they often found themselves in the vicinity of the Phoenicians, from the area of modern Lebanon. The Greeks knew the Phoenicians well. They had already divided the island of Cyprus, which they settled as the palace societies collapsed, between themselves and the Phoenicians, and were also learning how to adapt the Phoenician alphabet so that it could represent their own language. The Phoenicians were themselves in the marching line of a monstrous state that was again beginning to drive to the west, into the area of Syria from the lands of northern Iraq. This state was Assyria.[3]

In the sixty years from 883 to 824 two Assyrian kings had extended their power to the west. With the death of the second of these kings, Shalmaneser II, the Assyrian regime had collapsed in upon itself, but the impact of their campaigns (which featured repulsive acts of butchery) sounded a wake-up call throughout western Asia Minor. A new state began to coalesce around Gordion in what is now western Turkey, and states throughout northern Syria began to expand their power. It is against this background that we may see greater demand for the raw materials of war such as tin, or simply the profits that could be made through trade. It is one of the great ironies of world history that the rise of one of the most noxious polities in the history of this planet should spark the development of the states that would give rise to our concepts of individual dignity and human freedom.

The rise of Assyria may have sparked the economic expansion that shook Greece out of its post-palatial slump – powerful Greek states tended to require powerful (and rich) neighbours in the east to realize their potential – but it did not immediately create the circumstances under which athletics could move from the funereal to the cultic. For this to happen the aristocrats who dominated the sporting world would have to cease representing themselves, and start representing groups whom they would regard as fellow citizens. One striking sign that this development was under way during the eighth century is that sanctuaries become visible within developing urban space. In many cases these shrines are built over houses that had once served as the homes of aristocrats. It is in this context that the games as features of aristocratic self-celebration shifted to the world of public cult. It is notable that the vast majority of important festivals in the Greek world claimed to descend from heroic funeral games. While, strictly speaking, this cannot be true, it nonetheless reflects the memory of a process of transition that seems to have been starting even as Homer was singing. At one point Nestor mentions that the evil king of Elis stole horses that he sent for a chariot race.[4] This is again out of keeping with the spirit of the games most prominently on exhibit in the *Iliad*, but it may be the sort of thing that was starting to happen. And this may be why, at another point, Nestor presents himself as an athletic hero of the old school who raced his own chariots, then later as a grandee of the new school whose status depended on the speed of his horses rather than on his own skill as a driver.

Excavations at Olympia reveal that people began to frequent the site towards the end of the eighth century. The primary evidence appears in the form of wells that visitors dug to satisfy their water needs. There was, at this point, no stadium and no temple – only the mound housing Pelops and the great altar of Zeus. The cult itself seems to have been invented in the ninth century – there is no evidence of earlier cult on the grounds of the later sanctuary, and the supposed shrine of Pelops was a mound built over the remains of a very ancient (and long-forgotten) settlement. The mound, which was very old by the time people began to make sacrifices before it at the end of the tenth century, seems to have attracted people to the site. We do not know exactly why, but it is entirely possible that the original association of the place was with warfare. Olympia would long remain a place where people would erect trophies to commemorate victories in real battle, and there is some suggestion that there was an oracle there (useful to an aspiring general). Seen as an extra-urban sanctuary associated with victory, Olympia fits a recognizable pattern in the post-palatial period.

It is this association that may have drawn other aristocrats to the place to dedicate memorials of their triumphs (one of the notable things about the dedications at Olympia is that so few of them involve victories won by the people of Elis). There may have been a track that was used for foot races roughly where the track for the first stadium was laid in the mid-sixth century. Assuming that wells can be equated with spectators at games, then some sort of regular athletic activity probably began around 700, but this is not a necessary conclusion; major new temples began to be erected only around 650, and their cults, although linked with the idea of victory, are not self-evidently associated with sport. Given the association of the sanctuary with victory in general, it is likely that the athletic aspects of the gatherings emerged from this, and that early assemblages of expensive objects like tripods, which were symbols of aristocratic standing, need have nothing to do with sport per se.

It is perhaps most likely that the quadrennial athletic festival arose at about the same time as the decision to erect a brand-new, and possibly state-of-the-art, facility to house its contests: that would be the stadium. Assuming that the stadium was not constructed on the 'if you build it they will come' principle, this would mean that there should have been something that attracted athletes to the place before 550, roughly, and that might suggest that the games began around 600 BC. By this time there were well-developed city-states throughout the Greek world as well as aristocrats seeking to secure and establish their power in those cities – these were the people who would actually win the victories in the stadium at Olympia, and race the horses in the hippodrome. Perhaps 580 – the date at which the *Hellenodikai* were said to have been instituted – is based upon a real list, and if that were so, then this would be another piece of evidence pointing to a late-seventh-century beginning for the games – was the new office established in response to complaints about poor management? The first reference to the Olympics in Greek literature occurs in the mid-sixth century.[5]

To see the Olympics emerging around 600 BC would be to see their beginnings coinciding with the other festivals that would make up the great cycle of Panhellenic games. The traditional dates for the foundation of these festivals are 573 BC for the Nemean games, 581 for the Isthmian games and 582 for the Pythian. None of these dates stands on any greater authority than does the date that we have inherited for the foundation of the Olympics, but it may be significant that there is no obvious disconnect between the notion of a major festival being held in one of these places and the archaeological record of the place itself. In all of these locations there is a similar pattern of development – that is to say, an extra-urban shrine develops about the end of the eighth century and direct evidence for athletic contests appears during the sixth. At Isthmia the earliest phase of the sanctuary of Poseidon is datable to the end of the eighth century, while the earliest stadium (albeit hard to date with precision) appears to have been built in the sixth. The earliest dedication of an object connected with the games dates to the mid-sixth century. At Delphi, the oracle appears to have become extremely important towards the end of the eighth, when its wisdom evidently supported various colonization schemes, especially in Italy and Sicily. In one notable case it suggests a solution to some sort of constitutional imbroglio going on in one of the major evolving states of Greece.

Important dedications, previously absent, begin to appear at the sites of the games around 600 BC. The one outlier in this pattern is Nemea, where the earliest structures cannot be dated before the mid-sixth century: the shrine of Opheltas, which linked the site with the mythological past in the same way that the shrine of Pelops linked Olympia, was in fact a new creation of that time. But in Nemea's case, the site was dominated by the powerful state of Argos, which became a player in Peloponnesian politics in the later part of the seventh century. With two other major sites within a hundred miles, is it plausible that the Argives decided they needed a festival of their own? If they did, the decision would be both very similar to the choice of the Athenians, and better calculated. The founding myth of the games was set in the distant past and could be seen as one of Peloponnesian unity; it was linked with a war between the Peloponnesians and Thebes that occupied an important place in the epic cycle. This was quite unlike the overt Athenocentrism of the Panathenaia whose very title, which may be translated as 'the All-Athena Fest', proclaimed a self-promotional agenda that was less well calculated to bring people in.[6]

The archaeological record reveals trends and tendencies rather than firm dates and memorable characters. The early history of Greek athletics without such dates, or figures like the foundational nudist, is in some ways less satisfactory than one equipped with the comforting paraphernalia of historical reconstruction. That said, neither Orsippus nor any of the dates given for the games in the tradition ring true to what is actually there on the ground. A history of ancient sport that allows for gradual change as Greek society changed may be more plausible. It is more likely that athletics left the exclusive preserve of the *basileis* of Homeric society and gradually became attached to the temples that emerged either from the houses of the *basileis* or from the shrines at which they and others would congregate as horizons expanded and new wealth entered the Greek world. Such an approach may also help explain why sport became so important in that world, for athletic participation was not simply the preserve of the rich who could afford to make the trip to Olympia. Sport was integral to the upbringing of young men throughout the cities of Greece. Had this not been the case, then athletic victory at Olympia or Delphi would have had less significance than it did, and would not have brought the victor such status in his homeland. Without an interested band of independent spectators, the superstar cannot shine.

The great Panhellenic game helped shape an overarching sense of what it meant to be Greek, provided a forum in which the Greek states could meet and neutral ground where old rivals could come together to face a new threat. It is not accidental that the first meeting of Greek states, summoned in 483 to decide what to do about the threat of Persian invasion, should have assembled at Olympia. Yet the games are but one element of athletic life that coursed through the veins of Greek society, and it is to the place of sport in the urban and educational lives of the Greek world that we now turn.

PART 3
The World of the Gymnasium

11

Sport and Civic Virtue[1]

In October or November of 326 BC King Alexander of Macedon summoned his army to celebrate musical and athletic contests on the banks of the Beas, a tributary of the Ganges in northern India. Such contests were quite common in this army. Alexander had held games before laying siege to Tyre seven years earlier; then, a year later, in Egypt, first to celebrate his take over of the country and a second time before leading his army out against King Darius III of Persia. He would hold further games as he advanced through Tyre (where there was, he thought, an ancient temple of Hercules whom he claimed as an ancestor); at the Persian capital of Susa after he had crushed Darius; and again as he took his army in the direction of central Asia. When he reached that destination he would hold more games, but now in a new format. Our source tells us that these games were specifically of 'naked' and 'equestrian' events, whereas the previous ones had been 'naked' and 'musical'. Was the reason for this change that, as he moved into lands where the Persian aristocracy still held power, he suspected that men proud of their equestrian skills would welcome a chance of beating Macedonians in horse races, even if they might be loath to strip off their clothes and run against them? There is a good chance that no one was invited to engage in either pancration or wrestling, since Alexander is said to have despised both events.[2]

The games on the Beas would be unlike any of the others, all of which had marked positive turning points in Alexander's career. These were held, quite literally, at another turning point, but not one that pleased Alexander: they took place after the army had mutinied and refused to follow their king on a seemingly endless march to nowhere. So it was that Alexander erected monumental altars to Dionysus and Heracles – the two Greek gods who were thought to have invaded India ahead of him – and held his games to symbolize the restoration of the community that was the Macedonian army.

Alexander's games on the Beas, as well as later games that he would hold after his long and perilous march back to the lands that are now Iran and Iraq, follow in a tradition of ad hoc celebrations to mark the achievement of something great (or the end of something terrible). Sometimes they celebrated both, as when the army of some ten thousand Greeks that had followed a Persian prince into Iraq had found their own way home after a battle that had left them isolated in the heart of the Persian Empire, with a dead prince and a very angry Persian king on their hands. In an astonishing feat of courage and improvisation they made their way to the coast of the Black Sea, which is where they held their games.[3] The men who competed were not professional athletes, but soldiers. They had learned their games not as part of some sort of training exercise, but while growing up. In the fifth century, athletic training had become a feature of the basic upbringing of free-born Greek males whose families possessed the means to equip at least one of its members as a heavy infantryman (hoplite). It was in the gymnasium that they would form friendships and lifelong attachments, acquiring the habit of exercise that would carry over into later life. It is quite likely that they would have had their first sexual experiences with other young men whom they would meet in the hours of naked exercise that formed a crucial part of their education as good citizens.

The gymnasium was the central institution for the shaping of male identity in the Greek world. There was no comparable institution for girls. Girls might learn to read and write at home if their parents decided it would be a good idea for them to do so and, in a few places, when they were young they might have run in a foot race at a religious festival. But girls in Greece could not be citizens and neither could they control property (unless they were the daughters of Spartan citizens). Their exclusion from the games that their brothers and future husbands could perform in was a powerful symbol of their second-class status. Indeed, they were not excluded simply from participation in the games, but also from the audience, for it was deemed improper for women to gaze upon the naked bodies of men to whom they were neither married nor related.

The origins of the gymnasium and the introduction of the principle that physical exercise and training were essential to good citizenship cannot be traced to any tradition descending from the Mycenaean world, or even to the forces that helped shape the nascent cycle of athletic festivals towards the beginning of the sixth century. The skills taught in the gymnasium went far beyond training for an individual sport, and are intimately related to the development of societies that could be governed by corporate bodies of notional equals. To be a true equal a person had to be able to participate on an equal footing with his peers in religious rites, as a voter, a juror, and, as necessary, as a warrior. In a world such as seventh- to sixth-century Greece, preparation for these activities consisted primarily of physical and musical training. There was not, initially, any great need to be literate. Thus it is that while there is a good deal of evidence for the development of athletic infrastructure in the seventh to sixth centuries, the earliest evidence for public instruction in the literary arts does not appear until the end of this period.[4]

In the development of athletic institutions for the young there were two models that remained relatively constant over time. One involved a lawgiver laying down a set of prescriptions for how children should be brought up – asserting essentially that the state had an interest in the subject. The other model involved the autonomous development of places for shared exercise that were gradually taken over by the state, while leaving room for those who wanted to exercise on their own. Athens and Sparta tend in this, as in so much else, to diverge, each exemplifying the possibilities of one system rather than the other.

Spartans believed that their system of state training for young men derived from the decisions of a great lawgiver – they generally identified him as one Lycurgus – who created their constitution in the eighth century. One of the interesting aspects of the Spartan curriculum was that this training was plainly not intended to produce first-rate Olympic athletes (the Olympics probably did not exist when the Spartan system came into operation). This is not to say that the Spartans did not aspire to win at venues like Olympia, but such contests were an add-on to the typical activities of a Spartan. Thus Spartans did compete in the great games – there is some evidence for a number of Spartan victors at the Panathenaic games in the time of the Pisistratid tyrants, and for a number of Olympic victories. In the fourth century BC, when Sparta had become for a time the most powerful state in Greece, some of these victories came in the *tethrippon*. The only woman to win a major event, again the *tethrippon*, at Olympia was Cyniska, the sister of

Agesilaus, king of Sparta in the first half of the fourth century. She did so in both 396 and 392.[5]

It is quite likely that the Spartan tradition is substantially correct. Although we cannot date this event with any precision – the Spartans suggest that it took place roughly when the Olympic games were founded – it is hard to imagine how the Spartan state could ever have operated without public training. The principle of Spartan organization was that a group of citizens – the *homoioi*, or 'equals' – would defend the community and vote on matters of common interest at regularly scheduled public meetings. Political leadership would be vested in two *basileis* – most likely members of the dominant families in two of the villages that had united to form the Spartan state – and a council of elders. The 'equals' would be enabled to devote themselves to community defence and governance because most of the male population would be required to pay over a substantial portion of their income to the state, which would then redistribute it to the 'equals', each of whom would be granted a hereditary share, or *klêros*, in the community. Given that the equals could justify their existence only through total commitment to the state, it is not improbable that they realized they would have to subject their children to rigorous training so that they could take their place in the festivals, assemblies and battle lines. Several of the games they learned do not have specific parallels elsewhere in Greece, in that they stressed team virtues – one sport seems to have been a team brawl, another was possibly a ball game played with sticks similar to the modern game of hockey. That this sort of educational system was introduced in Sparta at some point in the mid-seventh century may reasonably be deduced from the fact that the area where the educational activities took place was known in the classical period as the *dromos*, or 'track', rather than the gymnasium (a gymnasium could not have been founded before the practice of athletic nudity began).[6]

Although evidence for the Spartan educational system in its earliest phase is extremely limited – all we really know is contained in a single paragraph composed in the mid-fourth century BC – it appears that male children entered the system when they moved away from home at the age of fourteen to live with other sons of equals. They would continue to live with their age mates until the end of their twentieth year. At that point they would be enrolled in a common mess, which would be their primary home until they reached thirty. Within the system, it appears, boys were broken up into three categories: the *paides*, 'boys', the *paidiskoi*, 'teenagers' and the *hêbontes*, 'young men'. In the Spartan view one did not reach full adulthood, becoming then an *akmazon*, until the age of thirty. It was when they became *hebontes* around the age of twenty that young men would undertake military service.[7]

Xenophon, the author of the aforementioned paragraph, thought that the years of flagellation, skimpy rations and inadequate clothing that were the lot of the young Spartans bred in them an admirable sense of obedience. He presumably thought as well that an education consisting almost entirely of instruction in singing and dancing, plus athletic competition and military drill, was sufficient – he certainly does not suggest that creating generations of physically abused semiliterates was a bad thing. Contemporaries of Xenophon were less generous in their estimates of Spartan attainment, suggesting that Spartans were uncivil and unsophisticated. All would agree, however, that the instruction provided was a relatively small-scale undertaking limited to members of the elite, and there is some evidence to suggest that it was somewhat less brutal than Xenophon presents it. In all it seems there were about eighty people finishing their education and joining the army as regular soldiers every year, and that parents continued to take a close interest in what their children were doing.[8]

Social relations that could shape the future of a Spartan were formed in the years of education; the boys were expected to take young men as lovers when they became *paidiskoi*. Their older lovers, known as *eispnêleis*, or inspirers, would be boys who had become *hêbontes* ahead of them and were entering the years of regular military service (they would also be expected to be taking wives), and it seems likely that these relationships, which were certainly assumed to involve both sexual and emotional bonds, were limited to boys in their late teens and early twenties. Xenophon, who disapproved very strongly of relationships between older men and boys, nonetheless seems to have felt that Spartan relationships were a good thing. What a *paidiskos* might also expect to receive from his older lover was instruction on how to handle himself, and, possibly, some instruction in letters.

Athens was very different. The crucial step in establishing a broad-based definition of citizenship does not seem to have been taken there until the early sixth century, when the great reformer Solon abolished a status known as 'hektemorage' by which a fairly substantial proportion of Athenians had to pay one-sixth of their annual income to some other entity (quite possibly the state, for Athenian hektemorage may be a development of some institution akin to that of the helots in Sparta). What this meant was that all adult Athenian males who could be admitted to one of the four tribes into which Athenian citizens were divided now stood on an equal footing. Solon also instituted divisions amongst the Athenians whereby the duties each could be called upon to perform were distributed according to personal wealth – those with greater wealth were expected to provide greater service, whether as political leaders or in assuming religious offices, paying for state services (including festivals) or fighting.

In the mid-sixth century – the period when the Athenian state was dominated by the tyrant Pisistratus' family – there is reason to believe that public support was given to areas for group exercise. There is archaeological evidence for a race-track, possibly used in the Panathenaic games in the place that was becoming the civic centre, the Agora. The earliest of these was a shrine to a hero named Hacedemus located to the northwest of the Agora (an area later known as the Academy). It was here that the torch races that were part of the Panathenaia had their starting point, and it seems to have become a place where people wishing to exercise would assemble. We are told that a male lover of Pisistratus (or his son) erected an altar to Eros at the limits of the gymnasium there, and that a contemporary of the Pisistratids named Cleisthenes (the tyrant of Sicyon in the northern Peloponnese) had established a *palaestra* (wrestling ground) and *dromos* (here meaning 'race-track') 'for the people'. Back at Athens, Cimon, a powerful politician and a famous general, enhanced the Academy in the mid-fifth century by adding 'clear race-tracks' surrounded by a covered walkway, and planted a grove to make the place more pleasant.[9]

Cimon's gift of an enhanced athletic facility to the people of Athens is somewhat problematic in that it presumes there was also some way to maintain it. Plutarch, our second-century AD source for this fifth-century BC moment, notes that what Cimon did was to open his private resources to the public. This is not perhaps an inherently improbable thing for a politician of the fifth century to do, but it does raise some questions. The dyspeptic author of an account of the Athenian constitution in the 420s BC (the work is attributed to Xenophon in the manuscript tradition, perhaps rightly so) states that in his time the Athenian people were constructing baths, changing-rooms and *palaestrae* that anyone could use to supplement the 'gymnasia, baths and changing-rooms' that the wealthy had been accustomed to build for their own use.[10] He goes on to observe that 'the mob' enjoyed these more than did the rich. The point is an interesting one because under-age boys do not really qualify as the 'mob' in Greek thought (no matter how the reality of the situation might seem now). This statement, as well as Plutarch's inclusion of the Academy, as improved by Cimon, amongst the 'meeting places' that were enhanced, suggests that whatever was done at this point was not done with a view to promoting some sort of coherent educational system. These seem to have been buildings for adults. It may be precisely because they were places where men would be found at their leisure that teachers of higher learning would regularly appear there. The philosopher Plato would lecture in the Academy and not, it seems, because he was eager to meet teenagers, but rather because that is where he would meet adults with time on their hands.

Even if one tended to spend one's time at the gymnasium talking to one's friends, it was still a good idea for the average Athenian to keep himself in decent shape. He was expected, if he had the money, to serve as a hoplite, and if he did not have that much money, to serve as a rower in the galleys of Athens' powerful navy; despite the image of bound galley-slaves popularized by *Ben Hur*, ancient fleets were rowed by free men. The requirement for military service began at the age of eighteen for able-bodied Athenian citizens. For the first two years, boys (now classified as ephebes) would be assigned to garrison duty in Attica, the region dominated by Athens. From the age of twenty they became 'men', a category in which they would remain until they were fifty, and which made them liable for deployment abroad. From fifty-one to sixty they formed a reserve. There was no specialized training before enrolment, but the fact that the eighteen-year-olds who presented themselves were expected to do so in the nude to prove that they were physically capable of military service suggests that they were expected to get in shape.

Another very important public activity for which decent physical conditioning was a desideratum was performance in the chorus and the races that were organized around public festivals each year. The races were relays pitting teams from each of the tribes – of which there would be ten after a constitutional reform in 508/7 – against each other, while the most prominent dance, the Pyrrhic, involved a chorus of dancers attired as if for the *hoplitodromos* (with the addition of a spear). These events were designed to create a sense of group solidarity within the tribes, whose members would often also be seeing military service together in an army whose organization was likewise based on the city's tribal structure. It is perhaps significant that the officials charged with organizing these groups were called tte gymnasiarchs. There were between thirty and fifty of them each year (the higher number in years when the Panathenaic festival was celebrated), and hundreds of fit young Athenians were also required as performers each year for these celebrations.[11]

The facilities that Cimon donated or Xenophon (if it *is* Xenophon) whined about are signs that the Athenians relied on a free-market system whereby members of the elite competed with each other to provide for the needs of their citizens (sometimes with a good grace, sometimes only when efforts to dodge those public services had failed). It was up to Athenians of all classes to choose whether or not they educated their children: it was not essential that one be able to read or write to function in Athenian society, any more than it was necessary that one know how to throw a discus. Athletic participation was thus always an optional activity and one that was de facto limited to those who had the leisure for training. But the words that Thucydides memorably places in the mouth of Pericles make it plain that the social pressure to participate in public activities and conform to norms of involvement was intense. For Thucydides' Pericles says:

Our love of what is beautiful does not lead to extravagance; our love of the things of the mind does not make us soft. We regard wealth as something to be properly used, rather than as something to boast about. As for poverty, no one need be ashamed to admit it: the real shame is in not taking practical measures to escape from it. Here each individual is interested not only in his own but in the affairs of the state as well: even those who are mostly occupied with their own business are extremely well-informed on general politics: we do not say that a man who takes no interest in politics is a man who minds his own business; we say he has no business here at all. (*The Peloponnesian War* 2.40.1–2, tr. Warner)

Xenophon, similarly, has his version of the great philosopher Socrates (a less intellectual character than the Socrates portrayed by his contemporary, Plato) tell a young man that it is his duty to the state to stay in shape:

Just because military training is not publicly recognized by the state, you must not make that an excuse for being any less careful in taking care of yourself. For you may rest assured that there is no kind of contest, and no undertaking in which you will be the worse off by keeping your body in better shape. (*Memorabilia* 3.12.5, tr. Marchant, slightly adapted).

The fact that athletic training was not officially required of young men does not mean that people were not concerned about what went on in the gymnasium, and the number of these public institutions expanded during the fifth century BC. The gymnasium at the Academy was joined, before the end of that century, by another at the shrine of Apollo Lycaeus to the east of the Agora, in the area now occupied by Athens' National Garden. Exercise grounds may have been established here by the late 500s, and permanent buildings to match those of the Academy were constructed during the next century by Pericles, Cimon's rival for political supremacy. The Apollo Lycaeus (the Lycaeum) also served as an important training ground for the army (which was paraded there before expeditions) and, like the Academy, attracted intellectuals of all sorts. The third gymnasium, also seemingly established as an area where people could choose to work out, was located near a shrine of Hercules and called the Cynosarges. It had a reputation for being somewhere the less socially well connected might be comfortable, and was where, in the fourth century, some intellectuals (especially the counter-culture philosophic movement known as the Cynics) could find a home.

What all three sites had in common was that they grew up around minor religious sanctuaries – there may have been statues, divine enclosures and altars in each location but there was no temple – and they were all outside the city walls (the Academy was nearly a mile from the city gates). The physical separation from the city is yet another sign that they were not seen, initially, as institutions for children.[12]

In the course of the fourth century these facilities seem to have taken on specific architectural forms that included areas for wrestling, covered tracks, changing-rooms and bathing facilities. It is to Plato's dialogue, the *Euthydemus*, that we owe the best description of the Lycaeum at the end of the fifth century, for he has Socrates say:

> Providentially I was sitting alone in the dressing-room of the Lycaeum
> where you saw me, and was about to depart; when I was getting up
> I recognized the familiar divine sign: so I sat down again, and in a

little while the two brothers Euthydemus and Dionysodorus came in,
and several others with them, whom I believe to be their students,
and they walked about in the covered racetrack . . . (*Euthydemus*
272e–273a, tr. Jowett, adapted)

The covered race-track mentioned here surrounded the wrestling
ground. In good weather people may have preferred to run on
tracks laid down outside. In addition to these facilities it is quite
likely that, as was the case at the Academy, there would have been
a garden set aside for the use of the *epistatês*, or administrator, of
the facility.[13]

The presence of the track around the wrestling ground ultimately distinguished the full-scale gymnasium from the simple
'wrestling ground'. Such buildings do not seem to have become
immediate features of the urban landscape across the Greek world.
Elis did build a gymnasium by the end of the fifth century for
prospective visitors to Olympia, and Corinth may have had two
(at least one appears to have been well established before its appearance as the site of a massacre during civil strife in 392 BC). Thebes
also had a gymnasium, outside the city walls, before 400, and
there was one on Delos by the mid-fourth century. The city of
Pherae, ruled by an aggressive tyrant in the fourth century, was
similarly equipped, as was Syracuse in Sicily. Otherwise there is
a limited amount of evidence to place gymnasia at Gortyn on
Crete, Oreos on Euboea, Byzantium and Ephesus.[14] It is perhaps
telling that the gymnasia at Delphi and Olympia were not constructed until the end of the fourth century or the beginning of
the third. No gymnasium has yet been located at Nemea, and the
one at Isthmia is likewise a third-century building. The history
of building types suggests that until the age of Alexander it was
the sort of thing that a place wishing to present itself as impor-

tant would likely have, but that it was not considered mandatory. It was certainly not seen to be a necessity at the great Panhellenic sanctuaries until well after it had developed in the main cities. The reason is perhaps not far to seek: the gymnasium in the fifth to fourth centuries was a gathering place for men who wished to exercise. It was not yet an educational institution, nor a venue for athletic festivals.

The gymnasium may not have been a place for the education of boys, as opposed to the philosophical speculations of adults, but it was still a public institution. As such it required an administrative staff and a set of rules governing the conduct of those who frequented the place. The staff included instructors for the various sports that people might want to practise (men who essentially filled the role of trainer or instructor at a modern gym or athletic club), staff to keep the place clean and the equipment in one piece, a vast amount of olive oil with which men could anoint themselves before exercising, and people to assist both in the anointing and removal of the oil. At Athens in the fourth century, for instance, the *epistatês* was a public official; the office of gymnasiarch, which would in due course become the regular title of a public official in charge of a gymnasium, was held in fifth- to fourth-century Athens by those who trained young men to run in the torch races at various festivals.[15] In addition to the public gymnasia, there remained many private exercise areas which tended to be run by a man who called himself a *paidotribês* (from the Greek word for boy, *pais*), possibly because he specialized in training younger athletes, or he was called a *gymnastês*. These men were presumably paid for their services by their clients, while the state paid for the staffing of the three public gymnasia. The fact that private gymnasia and *palaestrae* could survive suggests that even in the most democratic of Greek cities, people of means found the private option more agreeable than the public.

Whether they chose public or private, the state appears to have felt that young men needed moral supervision. It does not seem that the state was deeply concerned by the prospect that young men of the same age, give or take a year or two, might form deep emotional and sexual attachments with each other in the course of their training.[16] But there appears to have been a fair amount of suspicion that young men who went to work out on their own might attract the sexual advances of their elders, who might prey upon them. There was nothing to be done, however, about the occasional groping that would take place when the eighteen-year-olds presented themselves for inspection for military service – it obviously did happen, and people dealt with it. The state may have been even more concerned that the institutions it supported might give rise to behaviours that the average Athenian regarded as unseemly – chiefly the offer of sexual favours by a free Athenian male for money.

Thus when the Athenian politician Aeschines sought to attack his rival Demosthenes – who was in turn accusing Aeschines of treason in his dealings with King Philip II of Macedon (the father of Alexander the Great) – he did so by accusing one of Demosthene's supporters of taking money for sex. Aeschines' successful prosecution of Timarchus, in 346 BC, ignored the immediate political situation: that the defendant was a successful person, and that his political judgement was considerably more astute than that of his prosecutor. Instead, Aeschines' speech was directed against actions many years earlier when Timarchus had been a handsome regular at gymnasia. In so doing, Aeschines makes it clear that Athenians were painfully aware of the physical attributes of young athletes:

You know, Athenians, Criton, the son of Astyochus, Pericleides of Perithodai, Polemagenes, Pantaleon son of Cleagoras, and Timesitheos the runner, men who were the most beautiful not only of all the citizens, but of all the Greeks, men who had very many lovers of the greatest moral control; but no one ever criticized them. (*Against Timarchus* 156, tr. Fisher)

It was not wrong to have one or more male lovers; it was, however, wrong to flaunt one's sexuality. Indeed, Aeschines asserts that Achilles and Patroclus were lovers, but notes that Homer

keeps their erotic love hidden and the proper name of their friendship, thinking that the exceptional extent of their affection made things clear to the educated members of the audience. Achilles says somewhere, when lamenting the death of Patroclus, as if remembering one of the things that most grieved him, that he had unwillingly broken the promise he had made to Menoitius; he had declared that he would bring Patroclus back safe to Opous, if Menoitius would send him along with him to Troy and entrust Patroclus to his care. It is clear from this that it was because of erotic love that Achilles undertook the charge of Patroclus. (adapted from *Against Timarchus* 142–3, tr. Fisher)

These relationships between social equals were, Aeschines claims, categorically different from Timarchus' habit of seeking rich older men to live with. That was not love, it was prostitution, and 'the lawgiver' had legislated against such conduct *in extenso*. Or so Aeschines says, quoting a statute to the effect that if any Athenian should act as a male prostitute he should be banned from public life and could be executed; he had previously quoted a statute aimed at keeping boys under the age of eighteen away from direct contact with older men. It is possible that some such law existed, and had been included on the great wall of Athenian law that had been constructed in the last decade of the fifth century BC. Although the laws were in theory those of Solon, it appears that many passed in the course of the fifth century were included.

For the history of ancient sport, the prosecution of Timarchus is significant in so far as it underscores the Athenians' abiding discomfort with the notion that men found naked boys sexually attractive, that attractive boys could take advantage of the publicity of their lives as athletes to take financial advantage of older men, and that these relationships were seen as different from those in which, although the partners might be of different ages (such age differences were in fact typical), both partners were old enough to be considered responsible adults. Indeed, at least in the fifth century, artistic representations of athletes with their 'trainers' suggest that the two would not be far apart in age.[17]

Gymnasium participants in the fifth and fourth centuries were doing what they were doing by choice. The situation changed somewhat towards the end of the fourth, at least in Athens, when the city instituted a two-year training period for ephebes whose families were wealthy enough to afford the arms necessary to serve as a hoplite. This took place between the ages of eighteen and twenty and it was centred on the gymnasia. The point, now that Athens was essentially reduced to the status of a third-class power after its defeat by Philip II, was that the state would subsidize two years of military and civic training for those about to enter citizenship. The young men involved (about half the eighteen- to nineteen-year-olds in the city) would be expected to perform in the traditional torch relay races, and keep watch on the boundaries of Attica. How much of the day these activities would occupy is now unknowable, but it is significant that even at Athens where cultural life was a matter of pride, the training of the ephebes was distinct from any further efforts to improve their literary accomplishments. Literacy still did not rank with fitness as a civic virtue, and neither was for everyone – the state did not subsidize exercise for those who were not of hoplite status, and it offered no public support for literary education.[18]

12

Beroia

The century after the death of Alexander the Great saw immense changes in the Greek world, the horizons of which continued to extend towards the borders of India. In many of the cities that began to develop or embellish themselves in these years, the gymnasium became an increasingly important symbol of attachment to the shared culture of the Greek world. This world, now divided into warring kingdoms, was united by the principle that important people could read and write some Greek and that they exercised in the gymnasium. Even as the power of these kingdoms declined – pressured by the Parthian peoples from the fringes of central Asia in the east, by the Romans who were completing the takeover of Italy even as Alexander destroyed the Persian Empire, and by simple ineptitude (often the case in Egypt after the mid-third century) – the importance of gymnasia increased. There may be no more potent symbol of this importance than the gymnasium found in the city of Ai Khanum on the banks of the Oxus in northern Afghanistan. In a city whose architecture generally mixes Greek and Iranian elements, the walls of the thoroughly Greek gymnasium advertise a powerful link with the homeland as they display maxims allegedly uttered by the god Apollo at Delphi and arguably transported to the city by Clearchus, a student of Aristotle.[1]

It is from this transitional period that we get our very best evidence for what went on in gymnasia and how they were integrated into civic life. This comes from the city of Beroia (modern Veroia) in what is now northern Greece, then fast ceasing to be the kingdom of Macedonia. It appears in a text inscribed on two sides of a stone column from around 180 BC – that is, between the first major defeat of the Macedonian king by the Romans in 197 and the dissolution of the kingdom after a second defeat in 168.[2] The document does not pretend to originality – this is one reason why it is such valuable testimony to the role of athletics in civic life – but it does aim to be thorough. In so doing it gives a picture of the trials, travails and concerns that would occupy a person who had to make sure the city gymnasium functioned as it ought to. He was not in the business of producing Olympic athletes: it was, rather, his job to ensure the people of Beroia could enjoy good festivals celebrated by respectable young men who were in good shape and could defend the city if need be.

The text opens with the scent of scandal hanging heavy in the air. The people have assembled and a man named Callipus has said:

> Since all the other offices are exercised according to a law, and, in other cities where there are gymnasia and anointing with oil takes place, the gymnasiarchal law resides in the public records house, it seems a good thing that the same should be done amongst us and that the law which we pass on to the *exetastai* [supervisors of the public actions and finances] be inscribed on a stone stele and placed in front of the gymnasium as well as in the public records office and, when this is done, the young men will have more of a sense of shame and obey their leader, and their revenues will not be squandered since the elected gymnasiarchs will serve in accordance to the law and be liable to official review when their term is up. (*Beroia Gymnasiarchy Law* side A, lines 5–15)

It is a pity we cannot now know how previous revenues had been squandered. Did the young men destroy items purchased for them in a dispute with the gymnasiarch? Did he provide poor-quality olive oil? Was he falsely accused of providing bad oil, or of some other malfeasance? The most important thing that a gymnasiarch was expected to provide was the oil, and the reference to the (future) official review might be a concession to the young men. On the other hand, the actual law set out in the next forty lines is one proposed by the current gymnasiarch, and the point of the official review is likely to be a further protection – he is in effect demanding a full inquiry to clear his name.

The law that the gymnasiarch proposes is duly approved and provides for the annual election of gymnasiarchs along with the other public officials. Once a new gymnasiarch takes office he is to summon the participants together in the gymnasium and they are to elect three men (the specification that they be 'men' should mean that they, like the gymnasiarch, will be over thirty) who will assist him in monitoring the young men and the revenue.[3] The text then appears to specify (the stone that contains this portion of the decree is badly damaged) reporting lines for financial issues – chiefly the provision of the all-important olive oil, the handling of money from fines, and cutting the wood that will heat the baths in what is clearly meant to be a high-class establishment. This is where the text on the first side ends. The second side deals with activities in the gymnasium itself; the first issue is segregation:

> No one under the age of thirty is to strip when the signal is down unless the supervisor should give him permission; when the signal is raised no one else should strip unless the supervisor should give him permission, nor should anyone anoint himself in another *palaestra* in the same city. Otherwise the gymnasiarch will deny him access

and fine him fifty drachmas. All those who participate in the gymnasium shall obey the supervisor whom the gymnasiarch appoints just as is provided in the gymnasiarchal law, and if he does not obey, he shall be flogged. (*Beroia Gymnasiarchy Law* side B lines 1–9)

There are two points of distinction in these lines: the first is clearly between people above and below the age of thirty; the other is between those who are members of the civic gymnasium and those who are not. We do not know anything about the other *palaestrae* in the city, but it is obvious that membership in one of those institutions renders an individual inadmissible to the civic gymnasium. Presumably one would join such an institution only if one were not eligible for membership of the gymnasium for some other reason, the most likely of these being that one was a non-citizen resident. A third point is simply that people take these distinctions very seriously (fifty drachmas is a very heavy fine, equivalent to about two months' wages for a day labourer).

The raising of the signal in the gymnasium is known from other cities as the sign that any male who wished could come there to be anointed with oil and work out – these lines clarify what is not clear from other documents, that the raising of the signal indicates the end of the times that the younger members of the community could exercise. The point of this distinction is made plain by documents inserted into the manuscripts of Aeschines' attack on Timarchus that purport to be part of an Athenian law (they aren't, but the thought behind them reflects what someone thought such a law should look like):

The gymnasiarchs shall not permit under any circumstances anyone who has reached manhood to enter the contests at the Hermaia; if he permits this and does not exclude them from the gymnasium, he shall be liable to the law concerning the corruption of free males. (*Against Timarchus* 12, tr. Fisher)

The Hermaia was the most important annual festival in a gymnasium and would have been strictly regulated.

The next set of Beroian regulations provides that the ephebes and all others under twenty-two, as befits their status as soldiers in training, should practise archery and the javelin every day, once the boys (those under eighteen) have started to anoint themselves. There is no obvious reason why the training should be restricted to light infantry tactics (in other places ephebes and young men were expected to learn to fight as heavy infantry and even cavalrymen), but it is possible that, in these years after the first defeat by Rome, full-scale military training was restricted. Such restrictions are not the only ones mentioned in this section, for here it is formally stated that 'none of the young men should mingle with, or talk to, the boys'.

When it comes to the training of the boys, the gymnasiarch is to ensure that their teachers show up on time every day (unless they are sick or otherwise detained) and that they do their jobs. In a line that would certainly have no place in contemporary institutions of public education, the gymnasiarch is ordered to fine a slovenly instructor, or one who is late, a drachma a day (an entire day's wage). If the boys or the instructor are disobedient, he can flog the boys and fine the instructor (or flog him, too, if he is a slave). Every four months the gymnasiarch would have the instructors inspect the boys, appoint judges for the inspection and crown the instructor who has done the best job.

The next section of the law lists those who shall not participate under any circumstances in the life of the gymnasium, and the extremely heavy fine that will be levied against the gymnasiarch if he doesn't ensure what is perceived as the proper degree of segregation:

> A slave may not strip in the gymnasium, nor may a freedman, or the sons of such people, a person who is *apalaestros*, a prostitute, a person who practises some trade in the agora, a drunk, or an insane person. If a gymnasiarch knowingly allows such a person to anoint himself, or after someone has told him and pointed it out, he will pay a fine of one thousand drachmas . . . (*Beroia Gymnasiarchy Law* side B lines 26–32)

A person who is *apalaestros* is presumably someone who has been stripped of his civil rights for some reason – Timarchus, for instance, after his conviction, was forbidden to take any part in public life. The other categories of person listed here provide us with the clearest statement that survives from anywhere in antiquity of the exclusive nature of athletic training in so far as it was connected with the ideal of citizenship. It is especially telling that even though slaves could provide services in the gymnasium neither they, even if they were freed, nor their children who were free, could aspire to the rights of citizenship. Some fifty years before this document was composed King Philip V of Macedon had written to a city telling its people that if they wished to increase the number of their citizens, they should do as the Romans did and allow freed slaves to become citizens. He could not order them to do so, and it appears they ignored his advice.

In our world, athletics have often provided a path for people with great physical gifts to escape economic hardship – though this was obviously a point of dispute at the beginning of the Olympic movement, when the stress on amateur status was similarly meant to prevent people from disadvantaged circumstances from participating. It was only in the twentieth century that equality on the playing field became a critical marker of equality (or the theoretical opportunity for equality) in society as a whole. A Beroian who approved of a socially exclusive athletic environment would certainly recognize (and sympathize with) the views of Pierre de Coubertin, founder of the International Olympic Committe, and would be appalled to imagine that, in his world, there could be a Jackie Robinson whose career came both to inspire and to symbolize movements towards racial equality in American society when he began his career in major league baseball. It is notable that solely the prospect of a Jackie Robinson is addressed here; the notion that a woman like the soccer player Mia Hamm, for instance, could even exist and become an iconic figure would not have entered the mind of such a man.

There were other Greek cities where the rules were less restrictive than they were in Beroia. Slaves are sometimes mentioned as recipients of olive oil donations at gymnasia. But there is still no suggestion that they could participate fully in competitions sponsored by the gymnasium, and there was a distinct financial disincentive to allowing people in. Someone had to pay for the olive oil. In a case such as this one, where it appears the money to support the gymnasium is provided by the city, the city would have to provide extra cash. That simply wasn't in the interests of many city governments which, in the ancient world, had trouble making ends meet. When we learn that slaves are included in distributions it tends to be because some very wealthy citizen has offered to pay for the olive oil himself.[4]

With the gymnasiarch's responsibility for maintaining the exclusive nature of the gymnasium suitably spelled out, the next section deals with the protection of the gymnasiarch himself. It is, in its own way, every bit as revealing as the lines that precede it about the nature of athletics:

No one shall verbally abuse the gymnasiarch in the gymnasium; if
he does, the gymnasiarch will fine him fifty drachmas. If someone
strikes the gymnasiarch in the gymnasium, those who are present
shall stop and prevent him, and the gymnasiarch shall fine the person
hitting him one hundred drachmas, and shall be able to file an action
against him according to the laws of the city; anyone who could help
the gymnasiarch, and does not do so, shall be fined fifty drachmas.
(*Beroia Gymnasiarchy Law* side B lines 39–45)

Who would want to hit the gymnasiarch and be liable to a fine?
Surely it would not be one of the boys; in any event disorderly conduct by the young tends in this text to be penalized by flogging,
while the assailant here is envisioned as a person wealthy enough
to pay a large fine. What we meet in this clause is the ancient in-
carnation of the 'helicopter parent' who has dropped in to complain
that his son has not got what the parent feels he deserves. The
combination of the large fine and intense anger depicted here suggests a person who was deeply involved in the athletic success of
a young person. One very likely occasion for a parent to become
upset would be in the annual festival of Hermes.

The festival of Hermes shows very clearly the values that were
promoted in the gymnasium. For this festival it is stated that the
gymnasiarch will donate weapons as prizes for contests in general
appearance, discipline and endurance for those under thirty. The
award for appearance, as befitting any event where subjective judgement was involved, was decided by committee – in this case, a
group of three chosen by lot from a board of seven regular gymnasium attenders selected by the gymnasiarch. The more ob-
jective awards – those for hard training – were given by the gymnasiarch. Such contests are known from other places (by this point
there were two at Athens) and reflect the general sense that the

gymnasium should be the place where young men learned the virtues of citizenship.[5] There would also be prizes for two torch races (weapons again), one each for the boys and young men. For these the gymnasiarch would select the teams, which would then be supervised by a board of three (one board for each race), who would provide olive oil for the teams in training for the ten days before each race. A separate group of judges would decide the winner. The point of these arrangements, which seem more elaborate than might be strictly necessary for a relay race, is that the contest was not so much about winners and losers as about demonstrating good citizenship. It also suggests that the gymnasiarch needed protection against charges that he was rigging the races, or of favouritism. This would, presumably, reduce the chances that an action for striking the gymnasiarch would need to be instituted.

The final provisions of the law concern theft (a civil offence) and financing. The money for daily operations appears to come from two sources – the city, and via the sale of the substance known as *gloios*, the olive oil mixed with dust that was scraped from the bodies of the athletes when they had finished exercising. Unattractive as it may sound, *gloios* provided a significant revenue stream. According to what seems to have been standard theory, it might soften, warm, dissolve and fill out flesh, while one of the great medical minds of antiquity (albeit one writing centuries after the passage of this law) would assert that *gloios* mixed with *patos* (grime from bronze statues) was good for drawing off unnatural tumours and curing inflammations. It was also good for reducing haemorrhoidal swelling. These qualities are owed to the olive oil, while the use of compounds including trace elements of copper from the bronze statues would probably have been effective, since copper has antimicrobial properties that can alleviate infections and it is used today in a wide variety of antiseptic products as well as in athletic uniforms.[6]

The fact of the *gloios* sales is a reminder of the crucial people who are missing from the Beroia text. Although those who exercised in the gymnasium were themselves responsible for mutual anointing and for scraping off the accumulated dust, oil and sweat after practice with the tool known as a strigil, those who had to be there to pass out the oil and collect the *gloios* were slaves owned by the gymnasium.[7] They might also act as watchmen to ensure no one walked off with the clothes of a person who was exercising.

While the Beroian law provides the most comprehensive evidence for the place of athletics in the training of citizens, the theory that underlies the practices here plainly has its roots in the Spartans' practice of the seventh century BC – the Spartans were even now reinventing their own. A few years before the likely date of the Beroia decree, Sparta had been battered into submission by a powerful league of states in the northwestern Peloponnese (the Achaean league) and compelled to abolish its traditional constitution and mode of education. Some forty years or so after the Beroia inscription, the Spartans petitioned Rome to be allowed to restore their traditional system. The Romans, who had recently destroyed the Achaean league, agreed. The revised Spartan mode of education, now known as the *agôgê*, would be a matter of considerable interest to the Romans, given their belief that the Spartans had been great warriors and were politically stable. These were qualities the Romans dreamed of possessing too.

13

Getting in Shape and Turning Pro

Physical education for boys in the gymnasium may not have been intended to be a precursor to Olympic success, so how did boys grow into champions? First, they would have needed supportive parents and excellent coaches. These coaches would be very different from the *paidotribês* who could be found at the public gymnasia. They would be specialists in their sports and in what might now be called lifestyle coaching. The job of the professional *paidotribês* or *gymnastês* (the two terms for 'trainer' appear to have been functionally equivalent) was not only to teach sport, but also to devise a successful training programme. In the age of Pindar, Melesias, who trained thirty Olympic champions, was himself an Olympic-class wrestler, and a wealthy enough man so that his son Thucydides (no relation to the famous historian) was able to become a major political force. Alternatively, the trainer might be a family member, as in the case of Diagoras of Rhodes. Pindar composed an ode commemorating Diagoras' own victory in boxing for 464 BC, noting that he was a very large person (he also won at the other Panhellenic games).

His two sons Acusilaus and Damogetus trained in separate sports – Acusilaus was the boxing champion at Olympia in 448, while his brother won the pancration in 452 and 448. It is hard not to imagine that the choice of related sports enabled both to train with their father while avoiding a potentially embarrassing fraternal conflict. Their much younger brother Doreius (also a noted right-wing politician) won Olympic titles in 432, 428 and 424. The young men's sisters each bore sons who would follow in the family tradition as winners of Olympic boxing titles, and it is alleged that one of them, Callipateira, took a special interest in her son's training. She is said to have asked the *Hellenodikai* to allow her (alone of all women) to watch him in action. When they refused she pointed to the victory monuments of her brothers and father, and the *Hellenodikai* relented. In 424 and 420 Alcaenetus, an Olympic victor in boxing, watched his sons when the boys were crowned (statues of all three were on view when Pausanias was writing).[1]

Even where the trainer was not a family member, the relationship was expected to be exceptionally close, and there may also have been a sexual aspect to the link between a long-term trainer and a very successful young athlete. Pindar on at least two occasions insinuates that the relationship between trainer and victor was like that of Patroclus and Achilles – one of those he was referring to was in fact Hagesidamus, whom Pindar describes as being 'love-inspiring' and inspired to victory by Ilus, his trainer. This might not have been tolerated in conventional frequenters of the gymnasium, but athletes who could compete at Olympia lived in a world apart, with different standards. The tunnel leading into the stadium at Nemea contains numerous graffiti carved by athletes as they awaited or completed their events – one reads simply: 'I won.' Many give a name with the word 'beautiful' after it – a significant indication of the way top-class athletes saw themselves and their opponents. It is quite likely that the athletic champions of these years generally moved in a world where sodomy was a fact of life. Iccius of Tarentum, winner of the Olympic pentathlon in 444, was obviously considered eccentric when he announced that he abstained from sex for the entire Olympic training period. Nonetheless, he was also reputed to be the best trainer of his era. Cleitomachus, famous for his pancration match with Caprus at the Olympics of 216 BC, is said to have left drinking parties when the subject turned to sex.[2]

Cleitomachus would have been better advised to leave the drinking party as soon as the wine began to circulate, for intoxication was more problematic than sex. That would have been the view of Iccus, who is the first person we know of to establish a training regime based on empirical principles. As time passed, it appears that practical experience led to discoveries that mirror training regimes in current usage, especially in the area of diet and exercise. The modern trainer is aware that the anaerobic production of ATP molecules – the molecules that provide energy within cells – causes a build-up of lactic acid that leads to muscle fatigue. To counteract this, a good trainer will recommend aerobic exercises, involving continuous motion, that will stimulate the development of capillaries to carry more blood, bringing with it oxygen and nutrients to the muscle. The same trainer might also recommend a diet high in carbohydrates – Tour de France winner Lance Armstrong, for instance, consumes between 6,000 and 7,000 calories a day when he is in training (as many as 9,000 when cycling up an alp), of which 70 per cent come from carbohydrates and 15 per cent each from proteins and fats.[3] The point of such a diet is to replace the glycogen burned through intense exercise.

In the generation after Iccus, a man named Herodicus (who hailed from the city of Selymbria near modern Istanbul) was the first to mix sport with medicine. Somewhat later a trainer named Diotimus wrote a book *On Sweat*, in which he argued that there were three varieties.[4] It is from roughly this period that the second book, *On Regimen*, attributed (falsely) to the great doctor Hippocrates who lived in the fifth century, was written. The sections on exercise likely represent the kinds of things that were known to, and discussed by, athletic trainers of the period – they noted, for instance, that people who jog manage to lose weight and tend to sweat, and that those who try to work out hard will be very sore: 'Men out of training suffer these pains after the slightest exercise, as no part of their body has been inured to exercise; but trained bodies feel fatigue after unusual exercises, some even after usual exercises if they be excessive' (*Regimen* 2.66, tr. W.H.S. Jones).

These early works were dwarfed at the end of the fourth century BC by the four-papyrus-scroll tome *Particulars of Exercise*, and the possibly much longer *Athletic Exercises* (*Gymnastikon*) that issued from the pen of one Theon, from Alexandria. Virtually all that we know about Theon's work comes through the voluminous writing of the great second- to third-century AD man of medicine, Galen. Galen was deeply opposed to people like Theon, who he thought trespassed upon the sacred turf of doctors like himself. Nevertheless, in the course of trying to refute his work, Galen gives us a decent idea of the sorts of things that Theon discussed. In fact, Theon seems to have given serious thought to the stages of a work-out and the impact on the body, while claiming that athletic trainers were as concerned with health as were doctors. For instance, Galen notes that Theon uses the terms 'warm-up' (*paraskeuê*), 'partial' (*merismon*), 'complete' (*teleoin*) and 'recovery' (*apotherapeia*) in the context of a work-out.[5] It is likely that it was when discussing 'recovery' that he included specific instructions on massage, recommending either a 'hard' or 'soft' massage after a work-out, and he seemingly expounded on both at considerable length.[6] In the discussion of recovery he wrote, with his rather quaint imagery:

When any fatigue ensues, for the most part on the next day, in those who have exercised in this fashion, a hot bath is most useful for this fatigue, warming the whole body so that this warmth, just like a bottle gourd, will distribute food that has been taken throughout the limbs. (Galen *On Hygiene* 3.8; Kühn 6, p.208)

Others plainly spent a good deal more time on diet. Galen comments more than once on the large amounts of food that athletes consume, claiming that they both over-exert and over-feed themselves. He is writing in response to the prescriptions on diet that featured in the writing of others, and of which we may get some sense from another work of the Roman imperial period (probably of the early third century AD) written by a man named Philostratus. In his *On Athletics*, Philostratus provides a summary of the kinds of things that could be found in books by athletic trainers. The work itself, which offers a brief history of the Olympics as a way of introducing the history of sport, plainly draws upon a wide variety of sources, and illuminates the complaints of Galen about trainers who presented themselves as masters not simply of the art of exercise, but of all aspects of human conditioning and wisdom.[7]

On the subject of diet Philostratus noted there were many views, but he praises what he believed to be the habits of ancient athletes who ate barley bread and bread made from unleavened wheat, as well as beef (preferably ox or bull), goat and venison. The choice of barley and unleavened wheat breads is interesting, for both have a very high glycaemic level, working rapidly to raise blood-glucose levels and thus speeding the replacement of glycogens lost through intensive exercise. Venison and goat meat are both notably low in fat, while ancient grass-fed beef likewise had a much lower fat content than do many modern commercially raised animals.

What Philostratus dislikes is the substitution of fancy cakes for unleavened breads, and the introduction of fish, both of which were regarded as a sign of luxurious living. Putting aside his ignorance (one that was widely shared) of the protein content of fish, he is noting that the substitution of lower-carbohydrate breads for higher is a bad thing. Elsewhere, Pausanias observes that Dromeus (one of the contestants in the games of 476 BC) introduced a diet with large quantities of meat, stating that athletes had previously eaten a lot of cheese. The notion that athletes would have eaten a great deal of cheese – goat's or sheep's, for the most part, in the ancient world – is not absurd in that both are also decent sources of protein. Generally, ancient athletic diets do tend to be much lower in fat than modern ones; modern Olympic diets generally consist of roughly 40 per cent carbohydrates, 40 per cent fat and 20 per cent protein, though this average conceals massive variation by sport.

Over the short term, a high-fat diet stimulates the development of skeletal muscles, but muscles developed via such a diet tend not to recover as rapidly from exhaustion as do muscles that develop in conjunction with lower-fat diets.[8] In the context of Greek athletics, this could have been catastrophic. Modern Olympic athletes train to reach peak performance for a period of several weeks, but Greek athletes would train to reach a peak that would carry them through the intense competition of a single day. Although there was some variation as between the diets of combat athletes, who needed to develop muscle mass, and runners, it is likely that the ideal diet described by Philostratus was the basis of many adopted by athletes. The advantage of very high carbohydrate consumption was that it could fuel intense physical activity for the relatively short time during which the athlete needed to be at his peak. In modern terms, ancient athletes were well advised to follow a 'carb-loading' diet. The description of such a diet as offered by the Mayo

Clinic in Minnesota mirrors almost exactly the demands of competition at a festival:

> A carbohydrate-loading diet involves increasing the amount of carbohydrates you eat and decreasing your activity several days before a high-intensity-endurance athletic event. Carbohydrate loading helps maximize energy [glycogen] storage and boost your athletic performance. (http://www.mayoclinic.com/health/carbohydrate-loading/ MY00223)

The benefit of this diet is that

> if you're an endurance athlete – such as marathon runner, swimmer or cyclist – preparing for a high-intensity competition that will last 90 minutes or more, carbohydrate loading may help you maximize energy storage for better endurance and delayed fatigue. (http ://www. mayoclinic.com/health/carbohydrate-loading/MY00223)

The nature of the competition – the multiple matches or multiple heats on one day – makes Greek athletics of the Olympic variety into de facto endurance events. Although the typical diet may well have included more than an average amount of meat, Philostratus is suggesting very strongly that trainers were aware of the advantages of carbohydrate-loading. People might speak of Milo of Croton's ability to consume twenty pounds of meat, twenty pounds of bread and eight and a half litres of wine each day, but the tale is wildly exaggerated – it would amount to 57,000 calories every day. But it might well reflect a diet split evenly between carbohydrates and protein in which the carbohydrate content would be increased just before competing. The fact that Milo was able to compete for more than twenty years would certainly suggest that he was not consuming a great deal of fat.[9]

Diet was one feature of training; conditioning, another. Both Philostratus and Lucian, a satirist who wrote in the generation before Philostratus, describe regimes that are very heavy on cardiovascular enhancement, and treat those regimes as representing training principles that were many centuries old by the time they were writing. Thus Philostratus tells of a boxer from the island of Naxos, named Tisandros, whose 'arms . . . carried him far out to sea, thus training themselves and the body', and praises other 'ancient' regimes that involved making use of one's surroundings – such as rivers that one could swim across, carrying great weights (he seems to have believed the story that Milo carried a bull around the stadium at Olympia) – in order to get fit.[10] In Lucian's case, the description of athletic training comes in the form of a supposed dialogue between the great Athenian reformer Solon (generally regarded as a man of great wisdom in the Greek tradition) and a visiting Thracian named Anacharsis, who finds Greek habits odd. At the time the work was written, Thrace was as much a part of the Roman Empire as was Greece, and home to an urban culture indistinguishable from that of the Greek homeland – but for Lucian the invention of a voice for one of the most revered figures of the ancient Greek past was no doubt amusing. From Samosata on the Euphrates river, Lucian was aware of the way, under Roman rule, local traditions were expressed through – and at times, in spite of – the homogenizing effect of an educational system based on readings of the Greek 'classics'.

Lucian's *Anacharsis*, as the dialogue between the Thracian and Solon is called, begins with Anacharsis' observations on what he has seen at the Lycaeum. 'Why, O Solon', asks the bewildered Thracian,

are your young men doing these things? Some, wrapped up in each

144

other's arms, trip one another, others are choking and twisting or lying down together twisting in the mud like swine. And, right at the start – I saw this – taking off their clothes, they put oil on themselves and take turns, very peacefully, rubbing each other down. (*Anacharsis* 1)

What Anacharsis has seen in the wrestling practice is very much what we too can see with the aid of a wrestling manual that has survived from roughly the period in which Lucian, Philostratus and Galen were writing. In its lines we can hear the voice of an ancient *paidotribês*:

Stand up to his side, attack with your foot and fight it out.
You throw him. Now stand up and turn around. You fight it out.
You throw him. You sweep and knock his foot out.
Stand to the side of your opponent and with your right arm take a
    headlock and fight it out.
You take a hold around him. You get under his hold. You step through
    and fight it out.
You underhook with your right arm. You wrap your arm around his,
    where he has taken the underhook, and attack the side with your
    left foot. You push away with your left hand. You force the hold
    and fight it out. – You turn around. You fight it out with a grip
    on both sides.
You throw your foot forward. You take hold around his body. You
    step forward and force his head back. You face him and bend back
    and throw yourself into him, bracing your foot. (*Oxyrhynchus
    Papyrus* n. 466)[11]

Further, Anacharsis has witnessed men wrestling in both a mud pit and a pit of dry sand, which they sprinkle on each other, he

THE VICTOR'S CROWN

presumes, so that it will take off the oil and allow a firmer grip; he sees boxers sparring, and 'others in other places all exert themselves; they jump up and down as if they were running, but stay in one place, and, leaping up, they kick the air' (*Anacharsis* 4). What he has seen here, with men leaping into the air and kicking, are pancratiasts in training, while those who are simply leaping on the spot are using an exercise similar to one known in gymnasia of the early twentieth century as 'knees up', a forerunner of modern power steps used to increase speed.[12]

Solon assures Anacharsis that the creation of good citizens through hardship is the point of all the exercises that he has witnessed, but then he goes on to distinguish the professional athlete from the amateur:

> Their enthusiasm for exercise will become greater if they should see those who are best in these games honoured and proclaimed before the Greeks . . . furthermore, the prizes, as I have said to you, are not insignificant – to be praised by spectators and to become famous and to be pointed out as the best of one's class. Thus do many of those watching who are still of the right age for training, depart in love with virtue and hard work. (*Anacharsis* 36)

Just before explaining the point of the exercises that Anacharsis has witnessed, Solon points out to his companion, who is now complaining about the heat, that it is physical training that makes Greeks healthy and leaves them in harmony with their environment. If Galen had been around when Lucian wrote this, he would no doubt have been moved to compose yet another book, such as the work addressed to a man called Thrasybulus in which he shows why this was not true – why excessive physical training made men unhealthy and why they should listen only to their doctors. That said, the

146

point of the specific exercises that Anacharsis describes betrays knowledge on Lucian's part either of professional training, or of handbooks of the sort that are likely also to have been consulted by Philostratus:

> We train them to be good runners, accustoming them to endure for long distances and making them fastest in short races. The running is not done on hard, resistant ground, but in deep sand where it is not easy to plant the foot solidly or get a grip with it since it slips away from underneath the foot; we also train them to jump over a ditch, if necessary, or some other obstacle carrying lead weights that are as large as they can hold. (*Anacharsis* 27)

Solon next explains the nature of training for the pentathlon and then the point of training in mud-wrestling:

> As for the mud and dust . . . listen for the reason why it is laid down. First of all that instead of falling on a hard surface they fall on a soft one; secondly, slipperiness is necessarily greater when they are sweating in mud . . . this contributes in no small way to strength and muscle when both are in this condition and one has to grip the other and hold him while he tries to escape. (*Anacharsis* 28)

The principle that Solon is enunciating here is essentially that of modern resistance training – that is to say, involving contracting the muscles against external force – which is now recommended for athletes who will have to exert themselves over a considerable length of time (or simply for those of us who need to lose weight and get in better shape). In the gymnasium, according to Solon, it would seem to be ideally linked with cardiovascular exercise through running, and that again would not be out of keeping with

contemporary best practices. Nor was the discovery of these principles especially recent in the age of Lucian and Galen. Indeed, Galen
believed that the practice was so old that he would tell stories about
how Milo of Croton conducted what was essentially public resistance training by inviting people to push against him in the town
square.[13]

The one sport where we see technique that cannot be associated
with dietary control and endurance is boxing. Lucian has Anacharsis
mention the sight of people knocking each other around, but it is
possible that such 'live' sparring was relatively unusual because the
risk of serious injury was so great. That may be why, both in the
time of Galen and in that of Timarchus, there is attestation for
slaves as sparring partners. Ordinarily, boxers would train by hitting large skins filled with sand or water, or by shadow-boxing.
Philostratus says that they should only practise lightly, and with
blows in the air. But when they 'went live' in practice it might have
been with a slave who would act as a mobile punch-bag. Otherwise, there is some evidence that specially padded gloves were
available for practising with one's peers.[14]

Although our best evidence for training techniques comes to us
only from texts of the second and third centuries AD, the way these
authors worked, feeling that they were operating within a tradition
of great antiquity, and the fact that Galen targeted doctrines that
were hundreds of years old, suggest that the basic principles of the
training they described would not have been out of place in the gym
at Beroia. In fact, given the nature of Olympic competition with its
intense demands on the endurance of athletes, it is quite possible
that trainers were beginning to develop at least rudimentary understanding of these training techniques as early as the sixth century.

Assuming that one wished to become the sort of athlete who
could be a model of fitness and an object of admiration, how might

one go about doing so? Plainly, the first order of business was to find a good trainer. Assuming that this individual was not a family member, it might also be important to convince him that he would be engaging with a promising pupil. To judge from the pages of Philostratus, trainers might be a bit careful about who they would take on, and Philostratus offers some general guidelines concerning the build of potential clients that draw upon the principles of the ancient art of physiognomics – the art of judging a person's inner self by his outer expression.

The ability to judge character was important because trainers needed to be able to recruit the best athletes so as to maintain their own reputations, just as major college coaches in the United States must recruit the best talent for their system if they expect to keep their jobs. The ancient trainer, Philostratus says, must be a good judge of nature, he must 'know all the signs of character that are in the eyes, through which the sluggish, the impetuous and the liars, the less enduring and the intemperate are revealed' (Phil. *Gym.* 25). The character of a person with dark eyes was thought to be different from that of one with blue eyes or eyes that were bloodshot. Moreover, just as hunters inspect the animals they will use to chase their prey, so too must the trainer inspect his charge with care to make sure that he has the natural ability and breeding to make good. The latter point might be difficult to follow up in the painful circumstances of ancient mortality. The average person did not live much past his or her forties, and it was quite likely that one parent would be dead by the time a child reached his late teens. This meant that a trainer needed a 'method according to which, looking at the naked athlete, we need have no doubt about the parents' (Phil. *Gym.* 28). The ideal young athlete was unlikely to be one whose skin was tender, whose collar-bones formed cavities, whose veins stood out, whose hips (after hard work) were loose or whose muscles were weak. If the prospective athlete should seem listless, should seem to sweat too easily or not at all, and not recover from exercise in a way proportionate to his effort, he should not be accepted.[15]

Once the trainer accepted an athlete he had to decide what he would be best at. He would determine this on the basis of body type. The prospective pentathlete should be neither too big nor too small – lean, tall, sufficiently (but not excessively) muscled, and with well proportioned legs and flexible hips. It would help if he had long hands with slender fingers, for that would help him grip the discus. Distance runners should have strong arms and necks like pentathletes, but slender legs like sprinters: 'They set their legs in motion with their hands for a swift dash as if they had wings on their hands; runners of the *dolichos* do this, but at the end of the race; they do not run the same way the rest of the time, holding their hands forward, for which reason they require stronger shoulders' (Philostratus *Concerning Gymnastics* 32).

A boxer was different. He should have large hands, strong forearms, powerful shoulders, a long neck and thick wrists. The hips should be well built, since punches could throw him off balance. What he must not have are thick calves, for these indicated sluggishness, especially when it came to kicking the opponent in the shin. It is not a bad thing if he is thin for, in Philostratus' view, that would indicate good respiration – though he says that this is not crucial because a prominent belly checks the force of blows to the head! It is not clear how he thinks this works, though a modern explanation would be that when a boxer leans back, his stomach goes forward.[16]

The people of the most interest to the Philostratean trainer are the wrestlers, and the massive Milo type is clearly not to his taste. For Philostratus the best wrestlers are slender, with necks of average length, good shoulders, well-muscled arms, strong legs and good flexibility. They should not be fat, but mobile, adroit, impetuous and agile. That Philostratus saw training and body type as the key elements to making a champion comes through most clearly in his statement that no one much cares in his day about physical differences between contestants in the *hoplitodromos*, the *stadion* or the *diaulos*. There had evidently been efforts before the mid-second century BC to differentiate between types, but from 164 to 152 BC Leonidas of Rhodes won a total of twelve Olympic championships in all three events. Still, conventional wisdom suggested that a specialist in the *hoplitodromos* should be a bit more heavily muscled than a *stadion* specialist, and that the runner in the *diaulos* should be somewhere in between. That at least may have held true before 164 BC, and even four hundred years later Philostratus seems unwilling to let the idea go completely, which is presumably why he repeats the information even while saying that it is pointless. He never tells us why Leonidas was as good as he was. It seems hard for him to admit that natural talent might count for more than the skill of a trainer, and he rarely mentions individual skill. That said, he does note that an ambidextrous wrestler from Egypt who learned how to take advantage of this physical trait, after receiving instructions from a god in a dream, was a special case; and in another work, he shows some interest in the success of boxers and pancratiasts who received advice on their sports and careers from an oracular shrine. One of them, Helix, became so famous that his picture was placed on a mosaic in a tavern at Ostia at the mouth of the Tiber river.[17]

It is no more in the interests of Philostratus, and the many who wrote about training before him, to admit that natural talent might trump the skill of the coach in determining a championship than it is in the interests of Galen to admit that a physical trainer might know more about good health than he does. Nonetheless, the strength of Galen's complaints about athletic trainers who claimed to understand good conditioning confirms that what we see in Philostratus and, indeed, in Lucian, represents the state of the art of ancient thinking about athletics.

It was a science based upon observation, and one that does appear to have been grounded in an understanding of the human body. It was also a science that demanded an enormous amount of dedication from the prospective athlete, as well as a great deal of money. It is thus not surprising that most successful athletes about whom we have some decent information from the fifth century BC onwards come from aristocratic families. At Athens, for instance, it seems clear that the athletes who compete internationally in the fifth to the third centuries overwhelmingly come from that social stratum, and add to that the fact that the most aristocratic Athenians invested heavily in horse racing, while men who are probably from families on the rise might appear in the naked events.[18] In some places, participation in athletics could ensure entry into a local governing class; but it seems generally to have been the rule, both in the age of the Beroia gymnasiarchy law and in that of Philostratus, that a person using athletic prowess to gain entry into a city's governing circle was already a person of means.

It is from around the year 300 BC, while the wars of succession to Alexander the Great were still raging, that we obtain a good example of these principles governing athletic careers from texts that were inscribed at the great city of Ephesus in western Turkey. In one of these were are told:

It seems to the council and the citizen assembly: Neumos son of Andronicus said, 'Since when Athenodorus the son of Semon, a tax-exempt resident alien in Ephesus, won the Boys' boxing at Nemea and was announced as an Ephesian, he crowned the city, it seems to the council and the citizen assembly that Athenodorus the son of Semon shall be a citizen of Ephesus, just as he was announced at the contest, and Athenodorus shall receive the honours established in the law for victors in boys' events that are contested with the body at Nemea, and he shall be proclaimed in the market place just as all the other winners are announced. The treasurer will give Athenodorus the silver established for the crown in accordance with the law. He is to be allotted to a tribe and a chiliasty' . . . He chose the tribe Carnaeus by lot and the chiliasty . . . [the stone is broken at this point]. (*Inscriptions of Ephesus* n. 1415)[19]

The practice of proclaiming oneself a citizen of the place where one wished to reside after the games can be traced back at least as far as the fifth century, when Astylus of Croton in southern Italy, who won the *stadion* and *diaulos* in three straight Olympiads (488, 484, 480), had himself proclaimed as a Syracusan to please Hieron, tyrant of that city. The people of his native city were less pleased and turned his house into a public prison. Ergoteles of Knossos, who commissioned a victory ode from Pindar, was celebrated as a man of Himera because he was in exile at the time of his victory, and the practice seems thereafter to have become common amongst athletes, who could move from place to place. The monetary rewards, while acceptable in cases like Athendorus', were probably not sufficient in and of themselves to support an especially luxuriant lifestyle, and the practice of giving athletes who won at the great games rewards – again, at least as old as the fifth century BC at Athens – does not seem to have been intended to democratize the sporting world.[20] Chances of victory were too slim. Instead, such rewards, which parallel those given to other notable servants of the city (as well as to prospective benefactors), may simply be a sign that international athletic success was generally seen as a way of enhancing a city's reputation – hence the statement that Athenodorus 'crowned the city' by having himself announced as an Ephesian.

The reason that athletic victory was so useful to a city was quite simply that the virtues of a good athlete were regarded as 'manly'. Victory revealed that one had these virtues and could thus be, as Solon says in the *Anacharsis*, an example to others. Victory could come about only through hard training – or, as one observer put it, if you wanted to win at Olympia you had to turn yourself over to your trainer, obey instructions, follow your diet, work out regularly, limit your consumption of wine and be willing to risk being pummelled. In Philostratus' instructions to the trainer on the sort of qualities to be sought in the different athletes, 'manliness' (the opposite of sloth) is plainly the overarching criterion for a good performer and can only be attained through rigorous devotion to training. Philostratus disapproves strongly of luxurious eating, drinking to excess, and sex. In this he was not alone, for mainstream thought held that self-indulgence, especially sex, ruined manly qualities, threatening to reveal that the outward appearance of maleness concealed a nature that was the antithesis of masculine – even the essence of a *cinaedus*, a man who wished to submit sexually to other men.[21] Since, as already noted, it is quite likely that most athletes did have sex with other men, it is significant that this is not in and of itself a definition of a *cinaedus* – one could be both manly and have a male lover. What one could not do was devote one's life to sexual relations with any lover, either male or female.

Assuming, however, that one was able to escape the temptations of the flesh and find a good trainer, and that one possessed athletic talent, the greatest necessity was to have the money to get to competitions and establish a track record. The great festivals would not admit just anyone, but there were lots of local festivals throughout the Greek world from the sixth century BC onwards where one could go to try and prove oneself worthy. Theogenes of Thasos, on his way to accumulating more than a thousand titles, stopped off at a great many of these places during his career. A stone pillar erected at the end of the fifth century in Sparta tells the tale of a Spartan named Damonon who dominated a local games circuit in southern Greece with a chariot team that he drove himself, while also supporting his son who won repeated victories in all three of the major running events – the *stadion*, the *diaulos* and the *dolichos* – as both boy and man. Often the two would compete in the same festival. Damonon records that as a boy he too was a winner in a number of races. The story of Damonon and son epitomizes the sort of family-supported athletic activity that might be possible, especially as every city was likely to offer some sort of competition that a young person could enter.

In some places it was also possible that the state would support someone who had proved promising, by defraying the considerable cost of attendance at a major event or ensuring that very talented trainers were available. The people of Croton appear to have supported first-rate wrestling instructors in the age of Milo, and many years later the city of Aspendus would advertise the prowess of its wrestlers by placing their images on coins. The people of Argos may have set the precedent for this sort of state expenditure when they began paying for race teams to go to places like Olympia. The practice, which began in the early 400s BC, appears to have continued into the end of that century, when Alcibiades bought the state team so that he could enter it at Olympia. Alcibiades' own entry in the games in 416, while technically private, had a markedly public aspect in that he appears to have accepted very substantial donations from cities within Athens' alliance while he was at Olympia. This was not charity aimed at getting a young athlete without means started – a sort of athletic scholarship – it was, rather, a calculated investment on the part of a city to enhance its reputation on the international scene as a place where 'manliness ruled'. Thus when we read, on another third-century decree from Ephesus, of a request from the gymnasiarch to the city council that it provide travelling expenses for Athenodorus for some other games, along with his trainer, we conclude that the city is supporting a known quantity and is willing to sell the right of citizenship to some resident foreigners, or freed slaves, to do so.[22]

Athenodorus had proved he was a good bet to bring glory to the city because of his victory at Nemea, as well as further victories after that (unspecified in the text we have). Since fame had to be won abroad as well as at home, travel was important to an aspiring athlete; it would be necessary to rack up a reputation in various festivals before one tried to enter the big-time events, and we are fortunate that an inscription dating from the late second century BC shows us just what that sort of festival might have been like. The text comes from the area of a famous temple in Lycia in southwestern Turkey, the Lêtôon, which was the meeting place for the league of Lycian cities. It comes from a time when the power of Rome was casting an ever greater shadow over the region, but when the provincial structure that would characterize the later empire was still developing. Romans themselves were moving into the area, drawn by expanding economic opportunities, and it is quite likely that there was some sort of recent military intervention. The southern coast of Turkey was a notorious haven for pirates, and the Roman state had taken upon itself the task of launching patrols in the area. In any event, the people of Lycia had decided to establish a festival in honour

of the goddess Roma (the personification of Roman power). The
events unfolded as follows:

> The victors in the contest of the Romaia established by the Lycian
> league in the year that Andromachus son of Andromachus of Xanthus
> was agonothete [president of the games]: Flute player – Theagenes son
> of Apollogenes of Sardis – Citharist – Pythion son of Pythion of
> Patara – The crown for singers with the accompaniment of the cithara
> was placed on the altar of Roma because of the failure of the contest-
> ants – Men's dolichos – Aristocritus son of Charixenus of Argos – Men's
> diaulos – Aristocritus son of Charixenus of Argos – Men's *stadion* race
> – Antiochus son of Menestratus from Myra – Boys' boxing – Epigonos
> son of Artemon from Pergamon – Boys' pancration – Artemidorus
> son of Apollonius son of Hagnon of Philadelphia – Boys' *dolichos* –
> Glaucus son of Artapates of Patara – Boys' *stadion* race – Menephron
> son of Theophanes of Ephesus – Boys' *diaulos* – Posidonius son of Cte-
> sippus of Magnesia on the Maeander – Young men's *stadion* race –
> Nicander son of Nicander of Argos – Young men's wrestling – Milti-
> ades son of Xenon of Alexandria – Young men's boxing – Pateres son
> of Diodorus of Philadelphia – Young men's pancration – Idagoas son
> of Antipater of Patara – *hoplitodromos* – Inachidas . . . the Argive –
> Pentathlon – Glaucus son of Menemachus of Patara.
>
> The crown for Boys' wrestling was placed on the altar of Roma
> because of the failure of the contestants.
>
> The crowns for Men's boxing, wrestling and pancration were placed
> on the altar of Roma because no one registered for the events.
>
> Horse race [colt] – Callipus the son of Philocles from Smyrna –
> Horse race [adult horse] – Gaius Octavius, the son of Gaius Pollio
> who announced himself as being from Telmessus – Two-horse chariot
> race [colts] – Peitho daughter of Macedon from Ephesus who was
> announced as being from Apollonia – Two-horse chariot race [adult

horses] – Demetrius the son of Demetrius the son of Nearchus from
Apollonia – Four-horse chariot race [colts] – Moschus the son of
Evagoras from Myra – The crown for the four-horse chariot race
[adult horses] was placed on the altar of Roma because the contestants were disqualified.[23]

With their absolutely gorgeous location, the Lycians plainly hoped
that they would have a smashing success with this festival – hence
they included the full range of musical events to go with the equestrian and naked performances. It was also inspired by the fact that
the temple of Leto celebrated the mother of the god Apollo and
his sister, Artemis (otherwise thought to have been born on the
island of Delos). They perhaps even hoped that their games would
become an equivalent of the Pythian games (they restricted entry
to the pentathlon and *hoplitodromos* to adults, as was the case in
the major festivals). But it seems plainly not to have happened. The
performance of the cithara singers in this instance would have been
painful, both to the audience and to the performers, for there was
a general provision that if a performance was dreadful then no one
could be awarded the prize and the performers could be flogged.[24]
So, too, it is interesting that the events for boys and young men
(even if the contestants in boys' wrestling proved disappointing)
drew from a wide geographical range.

There are only four winners from Lycia, and the winners in the
cithara, pentathlon and boys' *dolichos* are from the same city.
Otherwise the winners have all come some distance – Pergamon,
Ephesus, Magnesia on the Maeander and Philadelphia were all major
cities to the north. Alexandria is presumably Alexandria in Egypt,
while Argos is in Greece. The fact that four of the winners – three
in the men's division and one in the boys' – should be from Argos
makes it look as if this might be some sort of ancient version of

an away match. The same might also be true of the contingent from Philadelphia, which provided victors in the boys' pancration and the young men's boxing. That said, it is also notable that while the men's running events filled up (in part, thanks to the arrival of the dominant Argives), the same was not true of the major combat events for which not even Lycians could be bothered to register. For boys and young men the chance to win was presumably worth a long journey; for older men this was not the case. An athlete who was established in his career presumably need not have risked injury in the ancient equivalent of a pre-season game.

The situation with horse-racing is rather different. In two instances new arrivals (we may presume) are announcing their presence in the area with a ring of authority. Gaius Octavius Pollio is most likely an Italian businessman, while we cannot know what brought Peitho from mighty Ephesus to the relatively obscure town of Apollonia on the south coast of Lycia, or what her connection was with Demetrius, son of Demetrius. Were they neighbours who disliked each other, or ex-lovers? Whatever the truth, they both had money and good horses, and, like Hieron and Theron on the Olympic stage of 476, they had each won in their own event.

Whatever the degree of personal gratification the victors here must have felt, it is hard to think that Andromachus, son of Andromachus, from the beautiful city of Xanthus a few miles away, was altogether pleased with the event that he had put on. Two of the performances had been so bad that no prize could be given, the contestants in the four-horse chariot race had cheated (were there more than two?), and he had attracted no competitors in the headline events of men's boxing, wrestling and pancration. What Andromachus had accomplished was simply to provide a venue whereby visitors from afar, a number of them young, could pad their athletic résumés, and a couple of wealthy new arrivals could show off their fortunes. Despite all of this, he had seen fit to inscribe the results on a stone pillar, and it is thanks to this that we can gain a sense of how athletic careers could develop, what it might take for the travelling athletes from afar to make the leap from local gymnasium to Olympic glory, or simply, in the case of the horsey set from Apollonia, to be able to show off with the ancient equivalent of a country-club trophy before one's neighbours. Victory enabled people to make a statement about who they were.

For the soldiers Alexander led into India back in 326 BC, the ability to compete with their fellows was a way for them to celebrate their identities. They had fought countless small skirmishes and participated in more vicious sieges and massive battles than any other men of their age. On the banks of the Beas, as they celebrated the athletic triumphs of their comrades – very few of the thirty to forty thousand Greeks and Macedonians who were there could have competed – they were celebrating the essential quality of their army, their masculinity, their courage, their hard training and their endurance. Alexander may have hoped that this would make them think a bit more about obedience, and that the experience would draw the fractured group back together. His men did not know how to run, box or wrestle because they were warriors. But they knew how to enjoy these sports because they were Greeks and because they were men.

The world of the gymnasium did not come about because there were Olympic games any more than because there was warfare. It emerged from the very particular association between athleticism and personal standing that defined masculine identity in the Greek city-state. It would continue to develop in this way for centuries after the death of Alexander, in a world dominated by a state that he may barely have heard of. This would be Rome.

PART 4

Roman Games

14

Greece Meets Rome[1]

The celebration of the goddess Roma at Lêtôon occurred at a moment when the people of her city, Rome, were just beginning to establish a permanent presence in the eastern Mediterranean. It had been only in 133 BC that Rome had agreed to take up the bequest of the royal lands belonging to King Attalus III of Pergamon in western Turkey, who had died without legitimate issue that same year. The acceptance of that inheritance had led first to Roman involvement in a bitter war and then to the establishment of a permanent Roman province – Asia. Indeed, many of those who had come to the festival at Lêtôon had themselves recently become subjects of Rome.[2]

The creation of the province of Asia was indicative of the haphazard process through which Rome began to acquire its empire. The institutions of the Roman state were only formally democratic, power tending to reside with a relatively small group of powerful families whose members routinely held the major offices of state; and the formation of coherent long-term policy had proved elusive. Earlier provinces – in Sicily, Spain, North Africa and Macedonia – had been created either to keep out the enemies that had once held those lands, or as the result of persistent policy failures. The province of Asia was different from the others in that it proved immensely profitable, even though the decision to annex it had led to domestic strife as well as the aforementioned war. And although the domestic crisis would ostensibly be settled by a brutal act of political murder, the tensions that lay behind it would continue to fester and, a few years after the games at Lêtôon, would burst out in a series of foreign and domestic struggles of unparalleled extent and ferocity. By the time they ended in 30 BC the Roman Empire encompassed virtually the whole of the Mediterranean coastline, all of central Turkey, much of the Balkans and all of what is now France, Syria and Egypt. The archaic institutions of the state had now acquired a brand-new addition – an emperor – whose very existence would help shape the development of the territories under Roman rule for centuries to come.

It is near the end of this process, probably in 41 BC, that we begin to see the impact that all the changes were having on sport, for not only were the Romans arriving throughout the Aegean world in greater numbers, but the Greek kingdoms that had come into being after the death of Alexander had all been destroyed – the last of them to go would be Egypt, which was occupied in 30 BC. The increasingly fat and alcoholic Roman who wrote the letter that allows us to see something of these changes taking place, one Mark Antony (Marcus Antonius), would play a major role in those events. It was his passion for the Egyptian queen Cleopatra VII that shaped the events of the next decade, and went a long way towards determining his fate (suicide) in the struggle for domination of the Roman world.

In 41 BC, despite his physical problems, Antony was at the height of his powers. He had survived a series of political miscalculations two years before, to become the leader of a coalition of three generals known as the Triumvirs for the Restoration of the Republic, who had recently demolished their rivals at the battle

of Philippi in northern Greece. These enemies had based themselves in the eastern provinces, and it was to take charge of their
lands that Antony was in Ephesus, and here that his physical
trainer, the man who arguably had the roughest job of any in
his entourage, made certain requests of him.[3] Antony writes that
the last time he was in Ephesus, this trainer, Marcus Antonius
Artemidorus – it was Roman custom for a man who received
Roman citizenship as the consequence of the intervention of
another Roman citizen to take his name as part of his own – had
approached him in the company of the eponymous high priest
of the Guild of the Sacred and Crowned Victors from around the
World, to ask that this association be granted substantial privileges. To be an eponymous high priest of such an association
meant that one was president of a group dedicated to a god (this
particular association was dedicated to Hercules), and that in the
records of the group the year would be listed as the one in which
that person held office.

Artemidorus and the priest had not only asked Antony to con-
firm privileges they already enjoyed (such as the freedom from
import and export taxes and seizure, both of which were essential
if they were to travel), but had also asked for new ones, including
freedom from military service, freedom from being required to
take up public service in their home cities, freedom from having
soldiers billeted on their property, a truce that would last throughout
the period of their festival, freedom from physical assault and the
right to wear purple. This last request is particularly striking in
that purple was usually associated with members of a royal court,
and to award this right was to equate members of the association
with men of the highest status.[4] Taken as a group, the privileges
effectively removed top athletes from any specifically civic context,
raising them to a pan-Mediterranean level. Having obtained their

requests, it is not surprising they now asked that he please 'set up a bronze tablet and inscribe upon it [our] previous grants'.

Antony's letter announced that he had agreed to do this. The privileges he granted are substantial, and it is quite likely that the reason he was willing to grant them was that previous arrangements had been fouled up by some poorly thought-out legislation from Rome. In order to raise money for their armies in the recent bout of civil wars – occasioned by the murder of Julius Caesar on 15 March 44 BC – Antony and his associates had arranged for the Roman Senate (the council of current and former magistrates that, according to tradition, approved measures before the people voted on them) to introduce a series of import and export taxes. The bill seems to have been drafted in such a way as to remove exemptions that had been granted by Caesar. At about the same time Antony was dealing with the Association, the people of Ephesus were inscribing a decree of the Senate requesting that if 'one of the Board of Three for Restoring the Republic should consent to make known by an edict that he had decided that no magistrate should impose a tax on teachers, *sophists* [professors of public speaking] or doctors, and that they are exempt from taxes', then he should do. Antony's conduct in relation to athletes accords to the spirit of this decree.[5]

Antony's intervention illustrates a tendency towards the subordination of sporting and other cultural events to the needs of dominant politicians at Rome. In terms of the Aegean world, the process becomes evident in the first quarter of the first century BC as Romans replaced the local kings as the dominant political force. The precedent for intervention in the squabbles of professional Greek organizations – there were several for actors and at least two for athletes in the time of Antony – was set by the most unpleasant Roman of the first century BC: Lucius Cornelius Sulla.[6]

Ruthless, vicious, intellectually pretentious and given to drink, Sulla was generally a trendsetter. It was Sulla who had first decided, in the wake of his victory in a civil war during the eighties BC, to post lists of his enemies – 'proscription lists' as they would be known from the Latin verb *proscribere*, 'to write up' – who would thereby be sentenced to summary execution and the confiscation of their property. Antony and his associates had reintroduced proscriptions for their enemies at the end of 43 and may have seen Sulla as a man who got things right, as opposed to their former leader, Caesar, who had forgiven his enemies. The privileges that Sulla extended to actors – he very much enjoyed their company – included freedom from public service, from military service and from billeting soldiers, as well as from taxes and special contributions. At the same time he alludes to some previous immunities from public service that the Senate had granted, probably confirming grants made earlier by kings. It had been Caesar's decision to extend these privileges to intellectuals. In so doing he may consciously have been capping Sulla's action, pointing out that he, Caesar, was at home with intellectuals (which is not to say that he lacked an affinity with actors – he had one and it would prove important). Quite probably Sulla had also been the source of some preliminary grant of privileges to athletes, whom he had asked to perform at Rome rather than at Olympia in 80 BC, but these privileges were clearly not of the same level as those he granted to actors. Antony made good the difference.

The invention of new privileges required a man endowed with autocratic power at Rome. Romans like Sulla, Caesar and Antony had come to replace the regional kings as sources of patronage for the cultural professions. Here it is a sign of continuity with the past that athletes should be amongst the economically privileged members of the elite. This was a very different situation from the one that obtained for entertainers in Italy, and the actions of all three Romans in these cases reveal another important aspect of Roman rule: the tendency to adopt their subjects' practice as their own.

15

Kings and Games

The Roman relationship with Greek games is subtly different from that of the previous kings. Romans such as Sulla or Caesar could grant privileges as a way of demonstrating their beneficence and superiority over other Roman aristocrats: whatever else might interest them, achieving power at Rome was the primary interest of Roman politicians. For an Antony, a Caesar or a Sulla, the decision to grant such privileges was a sign that they understood the Greek world and thus were themselves men of culture. In Caesar's case this was true.

Although Roman aristocrats might view the display of cultural sophistication as an instrument in the tool-box of power, Romans had long been aware of the games as a way of communicating with a large Greek audience. A century before Sulla, the Roman commander in the first war that ended in the defeat of Macedon had proclaimed the 'freedom of the Greeks' at Isthmia, and a generation before that a Roman had been allowed to participate in the Isthmian games as an honorary Greek after a Roman army had crushed an unpopular piratical state in the Adriatic. This Roman seems to have been quite fast, despite his name – Plautus, or 'flat foot' – and to have won the *stadion* race.[1] Many Romans who had come east in subsequent years, like Gaius Octavius at Lêtôon, had tried to involve themselves more deeply, and many who had come to Greece to enhance their education had been admitted to gymnasia. That said, the leaders of the Roman state (even if, as with Sulla, Caesar and Antony, they were bilingual in Greek and Latin) avoided too close a personal involvement. There seems to have been a feeling that while it might be a good thing to patronize Greeks, one should not, as a public figure, seek to compete with them, and there was still a sense in the first century that Roman aristocrats who aspired to the leadership of the state should avoid behaviours that smacked openly of those of kings in the east.

The relationship between the old kings and the great festivals of old Greece had been developing ever since the time of Philip II, the father of Alexander the Great. Early in his career Philip won the horse race and the two-horse chariot race; one of his first moves towards the domination of Greece had been to take control of Delphi, the home of the Pythian games, and he exercised the presidency of those games in 346 BC. Subsequently friends of his held highly visible positions in the administration of the place, and one, Daochus, constructed the massive monument to himself and his family that still stands near the entrance to the temple of Apollo, the focal point of the average visit (the surviving sculptures are now on permanent exhibit in the Delphi museum). One of these ancestors had won the pancration at Olympia in 484, plus numerous victories at other games. When Philip became the official 'leader of the Greeks' after defeating an alliance of Greek states in 338 BC, he summoned a council of those states to formalize his position, and most likely commissioned an impressive self-commemorative monument at Olympia. The Philippeion, as the building was called, was a circular structure near the temple of Hera (and thus in one of the most visible spots at the sanctuary). The shrine housed gold- and ivory-inlaid statues of Philip, his father, mother and wife, and of Alexander as the heir apparent.

Just before his assassination a couple of years later, Philip had entered the winning chariot at Olympia. Alexander used Olympia as a site for announcements to the whole Greek world. It was to Olympia that he sent a picture of his marriage to Roxane, an Afghan princess; and, in the last year of his life, a message announcing that all exiles in the Greek world should be allowed to return home. The value of the games as a place for the rich and famous to see and be seen is stunningly revealed by an inscription recording representatives sent to Nemea in the later part of the fourth century. The surviving section includes representatives from Cyprus who include the king of the city of Salamis (a famous admiral) and the king of Soloi (likewise a naval figure of significance), quite possibly a bodyguard of Alexander, as well as a leading opponent of the Macedonian regime from Acarnania in northern Greece.[2]

In the generation after Alexander it appears to have been the Ptolemies, the descendants of one of Alexander's generals who ruled a kingdom that included Egypt and parts of the Aegean world, who most readily continued to appear at the games as patrons of horse races. The first Ptolemy – Alexander's general – won the race for chariots drawn by colts at the Pythian games in 314 and 310 as well as a crown at Olympia. Ptolemy's son (also Ptolemy) won the *tethrippon* in the 270s, commemorating the event with massive statues of himself and his sister Arsinoe (who was also his wife). At this point the Ptolemies were presenting themselves as the true champions of Greek culture as opposed to other claimants to power in the homeland. One assertion made by their enemies was that they had ceased to be true Greeks – or such a claim would seem likely, given the loud representations made by their supporters that their successes at Olympia placed them squarely in the tradition of rulers of the past and of the recipients of poems such as those once sung by Pindar. Thus did the court poet Posidippus write for Ptolemy III (grandson of Ptolemy I):

> We are the first and only trio of kings to win the chariot race at Olympia, my parents and I. I, named after Ptolemy and born the son of Berenice, of Eordaean descent, am one, my parents the other two: and of my father's glory I boast not, but that my mother, a woman, won in her chariot – *that* is great. (Posidippus n. 88, tr. Nisetich)

Eordaea is a district of Macedonia – the reference to Berenice disguises the fact that she was born in Egypt.

The immediate royal family were not the only members of the Egyptian hierarchy to show their mettle in equestrian competition. Callicratides, the commander of the Ptolemaic fleet, won a crown in the *tethrippon* at Delphi because, the story goes, of a smart horse. The race was declared a dead heat (in a world without instant replay these seem to have happened quite a bit). For a foot race the judges would ordinarily order that the top finishers rerun the race (one way to cheat was to bribe the judges to declare dead heats, if remotely plausible, until you won). For a horse race the result would be determined by the drawing of lots, but in this case:

> . . . she who ran in the traces on the right, lowered her head, and on her own sweet whim, picked up a judge's staff, brave girl among stallions! The crowds with one universal shout drowning all protest proclaimed the great crown hers. (Posidippus n. 74, tr. Nisetich)

In 268 Ptolemy II's mistress, Bilistiche, won the four-colt chariot race, and the first running of a race for two colts at Olympia. During an age in which extreme flattery alternated with vigorous freedom of expression there were evidently some historians in Argos willing to assert that Bilistiche was the descendant of Argive kings (and thus a nominal relative of a Ptolemy who likewise, and with equal truth, claimed such ancestry). In this case Posidippus treated the event with what might be best described as an anti-victory poem:

> Plango has placed her purple whip and glittering reins on the well-horsed porticoes, having defeated the experienced Philaena, riding bareback, horse to horse when the colts of the evening have just begun to whinny. Dear Aphrodite, give to her the true glory of her victory, granting this favour that will be remembered for ever. (*Palatine Anthology* 5.202)

Plango and Philaena are the names of famous courtesans, while the reference to colts directs the reader to the courtesan who is good with young horses (double entendre). The references to her sexual achievements betray a bitterness behind the suggestion that the renown of her victory will last for ever – this would be true of anyone who was the first to win an event at the Olympics.[3] The ability to claim to be the first at something – even if it was only to be the first member of a family of kings – was still a crucial component of competitive glory. For an athlete, the possibility of a substantial royal presence at the games might serve as a valuable link to a centre of political power.

The attention that kings paid to games was not lost on cities, and as the cities sought to stake out territory for themselves in an ever changing political landscape, they would look to the creation of new festivals. Many festivals remained local *themides* (sing, *themis*) or 'prize games', at which the victors were awarded money. Others aspired to the status of *agôn*, such as the Olympic games, where the immediate prize might be an olive crown but the prestige was much greater. One reason to create an *agôn*, or to expand a *themis* in the hope that it would be recognized as a major *agôn*, was to signify newly acquired 'great power' status. This was why the Aetolian League in northwestern Greece announced games to celebrate the salvation of Delphi from the hands of a murderous collection of Celts who had tried to sack the place in 278. The new festival, called the Soteria (festival of salvation), would be held every four years and included contests in drama as well as choral and solo musical performances. Cities that wished to be on good terms with the Aetolians would then send *theoroi*, ambassadors, to the games to 'make sacrifice to Pythian Apollo on behalf of the salvation of the Greeks' as well as other sacrifices on behalf of their cities.

In 245 the Aetolian League, now a more significant player in the politics of the Mediterranean, announced a new and improved festival that would include different cultural events, horse races and 'naked events'. In so doing the Aetolians stated that their musical events would now be equal to those at Olympia, while the others would be equal to those at Nemea. In recognizing these claims cities ensured that the best musicians and athletes would indeed show up. In terms of their overall importance, the Aetolians might now note that with their Soteria closing in on the Pythian games, which they also managed, they had two major festivals.[4]

If a place was not so powerful, another reason to found games might simply be to protect what one had in a time of confusion, or to attract visitors to a local landmark. On the island of Cos, for instance, games were held in honour of Asclepius, who had a famous temple there, while at Miletus in western Turkey games took the name 'Didymeian' in conjunction with the nearby oracle of Apollo at Didyma. Political turmoil offers the likely explanation for events in the city of Magnesia on the Maeander in western Turkey. The city had tried to gain recognition for a local festival celebrating the goddess Artemis, claiming that they were doing this in response to an oracle from Apollo. The year was 221, and the result was disappointing. In 208 they tried again, announcing that the new festival would be an 'All-Greek' event to be held on a four-year cycle with dramatic, equestrian and naked contests on a par with the Pythian games. This time they had much greater success, and created an archive on the walls of Artemis' temple displaying the letters that had come in from around the world accepting their festival. The occasion thus recognized both the claims they were making about their distant past in Greece, and their present status in the world at large. A third reason to set up games, one behind the games at Lêtôon, was simply to establish diplomatic connections with a great power, or to say thank you for some favour.[5]

When it came to kings, the assertion of power usually provided sufficient incentive for any decision to spend money on games. In the eyes of the rulers of this world, political power needed to be asserted by displays of dominance. That is why the Ptolemies, and others, weren't content with displaying their magnificence at the games of old Greece or with extending recognition to the new games that cities might sponsor: they would also hold massive spectacles of their own. In 279 BC, for instance, King Ptolemy II mounted a spectacular display of royal power to honour all the gods and deified mortals who were important to the regime and, in so doing, initiated a festival to be held every four years thereafter. The description of the event that has come down to us from the pen of Kallixeinos of Rhodes describes astonishing floats, massive military parades and displays of treasure. It does not describe athletic events directly, or the musical display put on by an immensely fat woman that we know took place, but these are simply blips in the way the text has been transmitted to us, for we do find, at the end, reference to ceremonies for victors at the games involving twenty gold crowns.

About fifty years later the king of Pergamon in western Turkey defeated Celtic tribesmen who had moved into central Turkey in the 270s and commemorated the event with a new festival called the Victory Bearer (Nikephoria), in honour of Athena. The celebration, which was elevated into a full-blown festival complete with games in 181, represented the growing confidence of the kings who founded it, and helped build a sense of self in their subjects, who would continue to celebrate the event for seventy years after the last king had left his properties to Rome. The revamped festival also served to overshadow the claim to glory of a neighbouring king who had defeated those same Celts more recently. In 167 BC the Roman general Aemilius Paullus, having defeated the king of Macedon, held a massive spectacle in northern Greece as a way of demonstrating the reality – by now obvious on the battlefield – that Rome was de facto 'king'. He summoned *theôroi* from around Greece to attend these games, which included a grand procession, musical performances by the regional association of artistic performers, and athletes of all sorts. He himself acted as much the role of a king as he could manage, sitting on a throne and delivering judgements about the future of Greece.[6]

The display put on by Paullus inspired the king of Syria, humiliated by Rome when he had tried to invade Egypt two years before, to put on extensive games of his own.[7] The Romans might have ordered him out of Egypt, but he was still king in Antioch, and his display was very nearly as grand as that of Ptolemy II at the height of his power. In his procession, Antiochus included thousands of soldiers in diverse garb (some of them dressed as Romans), chariots and elephants. He even had two chariots drawn by elephants. In addition:

Eight hundred young men wearing gold crowns made part of it as well as about a thousand fat cattle and nearly three hundred cows presented by the various sacred missions [*theoroi*] and eight hundred ivory tusks. The vast quantity of images it is impossible to enumerate. For representations of all the gods and spirits mentioned or worshipped by men and of all the heroes were carried along, some gilded and others draped in garments embroidered with gold, and they were all accompanied by representations executed in precious materials of the myths relating to them as traditionally narrated. Behind them came images of Night and Day, of Earth and Heaven, and of Dawn and Midday. (Polybius 30.25.12–13, tr. Paton)

Finally, Antiochus presented gladiators, two hundred and fifty pairs of them, who gave exhibitions for thirty days. His gladiatorial display was bigger and better than any the Romans put on at that time in their own city. The point that he seems to have been trying to make was not only that he was the last great Greek king, but also that Rome served him rather than the other way around. His subjects, perhaps unsurprisingly, referred to him not by his official name – Epiphanes or 'God Manifest' – but rather as Epimanes, or 'the nut case'.

Royal support, civic pride or Roman imitation created, in the third and second centuries BC, a far richer world of entertainment than had existed at any previous point in history.[8] The range of possibilities open to an able athlete was enormous, as may be seen in the case of a fascinating character by the name of Menodorus, the son of Gaius the Athenian. He was a boxer and pancratiast who won at Olympia in 132 BC, as well as in both contests at Delphi, at Nemea, at the Panathenaia and a host of other festivals. His victories in both categories begin at major festivals in the young men's division, probably in the mid-130s, and then range across most of mainland Greece. He does not, however, appear to contend at all in what is now Turkey – probably a war zone when he was at the height of his career – and he never contends at Isthmia, whose games seem to have been cancelled by Roman fiat when they destroyed the city of Corinth in 146 BC. For all that Menodorus presents himself as a Greek champion, his father's name reveals that he was from an Italian background. He is especially celebrated on the island of Delos, then ruled by Athens, and it is very likely that he grew up as a member of the thriving Italian community that developed on that island in the second half of the second century BC.[9]

But what was the world that his father left behind, and what did the Romans do for entertainment when they were not setting themselves up as rulers of the Greek world?

16

Rome and Italy

The Romans had their own rich heritage of entertainment. These traditions developed within the context of a state dominated by a few large aristocratic clans that had united at some point in the course of the eighth century BC to form a community whose political centre was a valley between two hills on the east bank of the Tiber. Basic entertainments in the earliest Roman world included dancing in conjunction with religious festivals, possibly some boxing and wrestling, and certainly some chariot-racing. Participation varied according to the particular activity.

The head of any group in the Roman tradition represented that group before the gods – it was therefore acceptable, indeed mandatory, that the members of priestly dancing colleges be members of the nobility. The same was not true of any other activity, for the usual Roman practice appears to have dictated that the head of a clan, or any person aspiring to public prominence, offer a display of entertainment to the people as a whole. Roman aristocrats did not compete in athletic events organized for their peers, even though regular athletic training seems to have been expected of young Romans on the plain of the Campus Martius. The same tradition probably obtained in Etruria (now Tuscany), the important district to the north of Rome whence have come many representations of athletic events painted both on the walls of tombs and on works of art owned by the upper classes. As regards representations on painted pottery imported from Greece, it was conventional for the artists to put loincloths on figures who would have been portrayed in the nude in Greece, at least in the sixth century when athletic nakedness began to take hold. From later times there exist paintings in purely Etruscan contexts of performers who are naked, as they would have been if they were at Olympia.[1] There is no suggestion that these people were well-born Etruscans.

To the south of Rome, in Campania and Samnium, there were other traditions which would come to Rome only after the conquest of those areas at the end of the fourth century BC; and further south were the lands shared by Greeks and various Italian tribes that Milo of Croton had called home. It was inevitable, therefore, that as Rome grew more powerful in Italy, it should adopt traditions from the peoples who became part of the extended Roman state. It was perhaps also inevitable that whatever these traditions might be, they would be incorporated into the Roman scene in a way that would support the existing power structure. Indeed, the difference between Greek and Roman attitudes may be summed up most simply by the three words used for 'event'. An Olympic (or other) game in Greece was an *agôn* – a contest – while at Rome an event was either a *ludus* – a game – or a *munus* – a gift. The Greek term focuses attention on the experience of the participant, while the Latin words focus on the spectator, who is either there to have fun or to receive the present.

This distinction shows up quite plainly in some paintings and reliefs found in Etruria depicting spectators gathered on raised benches, thereby sharing visual space with the contestants (and, in a couple of instances, supplementing the action in the arena by sodomizing each other).[2] This does not happen in Greek art, where attention is directed towards the athlete and others associated with the event. Etruscan art also reveals that women could attend the games, again quite possibly because the performers are removed from their social world – they are objects rather than real people. Women would also be included in the audience at Roman games. In terms of the sports that were favoured at this time, it appears that what the Etruscans enjoyed most were boxing, wrestling, foot races, possibly something like the pentathlon, and chariot-racing, in both two- and three-horse chariots.

Although much of the evidence points to a heavily top-down structure, there is a certain amount that suggests the contrary. Some stories suggest that members of the Etruscan aristocracies drove their own chariots, and in the law code that was created in Rome during the fifth century BC it is stated that the only gold that could be buried with a man was that in the crown he had won through his own valour or in a chariot race. The law also states that this was not the case for crowns that a man's property – for example, his horses, driven by others or by his slaves – won for him.[3] In one of these depictions of chariot-racing, the charioteers seem to be wearing distinctive uniforms with conical hats. Such uniforms would be very much a feature of Roman chariot-racing, which is the one sport with a long history at the centre of Roman public life. Another issue may be a latent attempt to link athletic competition to community identity. On one of the oldest of the known Etruscan tombs depicting athletic events, two wrestlers are labelled in such a way as to suggest a contest between Etruscans and outsiders.[4] The sense that games could represent contests between communities (even though the contestants were of low status) would be a feature of the Roman world.

The reason the Etruscan evidence is so interesting is that, of the districts of Italy in the seventh and sixth centuries, the point at which we know that Rome was developing as a city, Etruria was the one most closely linked with Rome. The Romans even believed that some of their early kings were Etruscans, and there was a tradition that the Caelian Hill, one of the seven hills of Rome, was named after an Etruscan adventurer. One of the earliest artistic representations that we have of an actual Roman comes not from Rome, but from the wall of a tomb in the Etruscan city of Volci (the person in question is identified on the painting as 'Gnaeus Tarquin from Rome'). Thus if Etruscan aristocrats drove their own chariots, and there is evidence in a legal text that Roman aristocrats did so as well, there is no obvious reason to doubt that this is what happened.

So what then does the evidence for aristocratic participation in the games mean, and when do aristocrats eventually stop competing in person? Quite possibly it means that chariot-racing was caught up in the changes that the Roman state was undergoing during the fifth century. One of these changes was the installation of a government headed by a pair of annual magistrates in place of a king, another was an ultimately unsuccessful effort to restrict participation in the games to higher office, and a third was that members of the aristocracy chose to live relatively close together on the Palatine Hill in houses that were quite similar to each other in size and shape.[5] All these moves suggest that the dominant families of the Roman state were restricting venues for direct competition. If that were the case, it would make some sense that they stopped racing against each other, and turned entertainment over to professionals whom they could hire in turn.

Whatever the sociological factors that began shaping the history of chariot-racing in the early years of Rome's history, it is obvious that, although the Etruscans enjoyed chariot-racing, the specific form of it that took place in the Circus Maximus was a

Roman adaptation of the sport. The dimensions of the valley inhabited by these Romans determined the basic form that the races
took. Romans who lived in the time of Mark Antony and Julius
Caesar believed that races were held here before the expulsion of
the kings in the late sixth century BC.[6] But why here? In one of
those classic chicken-and-egg conundrums arising where there is
no direct evidence, we cannot know whether the area for the track
was selected because there were cults in the area that lent themselves to chariot-racing, or whether the cults were celebrated there
because of the races. One site was a shrine to the god Consus who
appears to have been connected with horses; the other was to a
divinity named Murcia who was a goddess of luck. The layout of
the track meant that the shrines of Murcia and Consus were both
near the far turning posts.

The early date for a race-track in the Circus Maximus appears
to be confirmed by the statement that a permanent seat at the races
was reserved for a man who won a famous victory over Rome's
immediate neighbours. The seat was said to be near the shrine of
Murcia. Over a century later we begin to get references to things
happening in the world of Roman chariot-racing suggesting that
what would become the classic form of the race – the chariots running seven laps in multiples of four – was taking shape. It is in 329
that permanent starting gates were built. The original name for a
starting gate was *oppidum*, a word that usually means 'town' in
Latin, suggesting they were of quite substantial size. This is important because there is a necessary correlation between the structure
of the starting mechanism and the number of contestants, and this
might suggest that the four factions that would dominate racing
throughout the centuries for which we have ample evidence had
come into being.

Our first explicit reference to them comes in the early second

century BC, when the poet Ennius wrote: 'They waited in anticipation, just as when the consul wishes to give the signal [*mittere
signum*] for the start, and they all stare with rapt attention at the
mouths [*orae*] of the *carceres* which will immediately send painted
chariots out from their jaws' (*Annals* fr. xlvii, 79–83 Skutsch). The
painted chariots are those decorated with the colours of the factions, and it is interesting that Ennius here uses several terms that
are also known from the later vocabulary of racing, such as *mittere signum* – the standard phrase for starting a race – and later
technical terms like *orae* and *carceres* (meaning both the barriers
at the front of the starting gates and the starting gates themselves).[7]
Ennius' reference to painted chariots suggests teams and uniforms.
This might take us back to the conical hats of the charioteers from
Etruria. It should certainly take us forward to the time when professional teams of charioteers contracted their services to a person
who wished to put on a chariot-race. I suspect they were already
coming to dominate the sport when the first *oppidum* was built.

Aside from the team aspect of the sport, another odd fact about
chariot-racing was that members of the aristocracy were directly
involved in the administration of the circus faction – these were
members of the so-called equestrian order, or the class of Romans
that would provide members of the Senate and other leaders of
society. The model for the administration of the circus faction was
roughly that which the Romans used for other important state
services contracted out to corporations of equestrians. In 214 BC,
as Rome was struggling for survival against the invading army of
the Carthaginian, Hannibal, we are told that the censors who were
in charge of setting the contract for the provision of chariot horses
said they could no longer do so. Those who provided the horses
said they would continue to supply them, but would wait for payment until the Carthaginians were defeated.[8] Centuries later the

censors were still offering contracts for the supply of race horses, and even members of the senatorial order were allowed to bid on them – they were banned from bidding on most other contracts, and it looks as if in this cast the process of contracting was so old by the third century that it was thought not to be worth changing.

Circus chariot-racing would remain a particularly Roman contribution to the history of sport. The two other entertainments that came into prominence at Rome during the third century had roots elsewhere. These were stage productions and gladiatorial combat.

17

Actors and Gladiators

Although not strictly speaking an aspect of the history of sport, the history of the stage is linked with that of other entertainments in the Roman world by the status of the performers. In the Greek world, actors and athletes were drawn from the same classes and could, depending on the event, be competing at the same festival. For the Romans, actors and athletes were likewise drawn from the same class and regarded in roughly the same way. They were slaves or immigrants whose primary purpose in life was to provide support for the political ambitions of the nobility. It is also true that, as with chariot-racing, there was a tendency over time to draw a sharp distinction between the leaders of society and those whom they employed. The earliest priests at Rome, for instance, tended to be dancers who were members of noble families. The fact that these priesthoods continued to exist for centuries was a sign of the inherent conservatism of Roman society, but it also indicated conscious decisions over time that new priesthoods should not engage in physical performance. By the third century BC, Roman priests would not even participate directly in the slaughter of the animals over whose sacrifice they presided. Performing priests were associated now with foreign cults.

When we finally, about this time, begin to get some evidence for the development of the arts at Rome, it is striking that routines such as the obscene Fescinnine exchanges or Atellan farce, a form of improvised comedy based on stock characters, took their name from other towns in Italy (Fescinnia and Atella), while the genres of *comoedia* and *tragoedia* were so obviously foreign that the Latin words are simply transliterations of the Greek. The most significant poets of the third and early second centuries BC – the period from which the earliest Latin literature survives – include the aforementioned Ennius, and Naevius. The latter hailed from Campania (the district that borders the bay of Naples), the former from the heel of Italy. A third major figure of this period, Livius Andronicus, was a freed slave, while his slightly younger contemporary, the comic playwright Plautus (probably no relation to the sprinter at the Isthmian games), came from Umbria in northwest Italy. The demand for their services may explain the creation of a guild of playwrights and actors, which could negotiate payment for the talents of its members even though it did not guarantee the security of their persons.[1] Naevius is said to have been imprisoned for composing some unflattering lines about one of the great aristocratic families of the age.

Naevius' most famous work was a poem about Rome's first war with Carthage, a titanic struggle that raged from 264 to 241 BC. The year in which that war broke out is also the year in which, Roman tradition held, gladiators fought for the first time in the Roman Forum, at the funeral games for a man named Lucius Junius Brutus Pera.[2] It is quite likely that the tradition is roughly correct in suggesting that gladiators had not come to Rome until about this time.

The earliest evidence for gladiatorial combat comes not from Rome or Etruria but from the south, from Campania and surrounding lands. Livy, the principal source of our information for fourth-century Roman history, says that after the Romans defeated a Samnite army that had been specially equipped with gold and silver shields, they dedicated these shields around the Forum, while their Campanian allies (who detested the Samnites) gave them to the gladiators whose duels they watched over dinner. When they did so they called those gladiators 'Samnites', an act that may be evocative of the 'team spirit' suggested by slight evidence for fights between 'locals' and 'outsiders' in Etruscan sport.[3] Evidence from elsewhere suggests that others might have acted differently.

The promontory of Surretum separates the bay of Naples from that of Salerno. Towards the southern end of the bay of Salerno sits the city of Paestum. Paestum's western neighbours were the very Samnites whom the Romans and Campanians were fighting in the fourth century, and its culture was heavily influenced by theirs. For this reason it is especially interesting that three tombs of roughly fourth-century date have paintings of warriors, fighting with spears, in what are plainly scenes of funeral games. In one of these paintings, scantily clad contestants are continuing to fight even though they have been wounded. Two have wounds on their upper thighs and one of these men also has a wound at his right shoulder. The location of these wounds is significant for, in paintings of later gladiatorial fights, the most common places where wounds are shown are the shoulder and the leg. Since there are no parallels for this in the contemporary Greek world (or elsewhere), the only reasonable assumption is that these fights have their origin in the nearby hills of Samnium.

The armament, as well as the location of the wounds, is significant in the paintings at Paestum because the term 'gladiator' implies a fighter who used the *gladius*, or sword. The problem is that the sword did not become the basic tool of the Italian infantryman until the later third century BC. The earliest gladiators, as these paintings suggest, are unlikely to have been 'gladiators' in the sense that they used contemporary infantry arms, which were, at this point, spears. It is interesting and perhaps of considerable importance that the Greek term for gladiator is *monomachos*, or 'man who fights on his own'. One of the earliest texts that actually mentions a gladiator is the history composed by the Greek historian Polybius in the second century BC, and he uses the word *monomachos*, quite possibly because that is the word that had long since been established in Greek, one of the languages spoken extensively around the bay of Naples and at Paestum.

The term 'gladiator' likely became established later in Latin when the bulk of the combatants started to use swords, which became the basic killing weapon of the Roman infantryman around 225 BC. Even then it might not have been universally adopted by those who fought for the pleasure of others. Early representations of gladiators show men armed with either spears or swords. A curious relief from the Sabine lands to the east of Rome, dating from the early first century BC, shows two pairs of what are plainly gladiators (in that they are lightly armoured), fighting with shields and swords and with a girl standing between the two pairs. Another relief, also of the first century BC, comes from the city of Amiternum in Etruria. It appears to show an event that took place at funeral games, probably those of a local worthy named Publius Apsius. The gladiators in this case fight with spears and are backed up by boys who act as seconds and whose job it is to supply them with fresh weapons.[4]

At Rome, the first display of gladiators took place at funeral games. The association between gladiators and funeral games is a sign that the virtues they displayed were felt to be intimately connected with the virtues of the living – just as the competitive values of the companions of Patroclus in the *Iliad* were reflected in the circumstances of the games that Homer inserted in the twenty-third book of the *Iliad*.[5] It is likewise notable that none of these early depictions show anyone being killed. The sport is plainly dangerous, but then so were chariot-racing, boxing and wrestling (pancration does not seem to have spread outside of the Greek cities of southern Italy). Gladiators themselves were surely men of the same social status (that is to say, low) as other featured entertainers, but they were neither criminals nor prisoners of war. It is striking that when Livy describes the banquets of the Campanians, he does not say that the gladiators were 'Samnite' but rather that they were 'compelled to fight' under the name 'Samnites'. At times other gladiators were called Gauls and Thracians, also names of foreign people whom the Romans disliked. The Gauls who lived in northern Italy and France were a constant object of dread in the Roman imagination not only because they were warlike, numerous and disposed to take sides against them, but also because a band of Gauls had sacked Rome in the early fourth century BC. The Thracians showed an unpleasant propensity to defeat Roman armies, once the province of Macedonia was established in 146 BC.

The tendency to name gladiators after people whom the Romans did not like may be a sign, again, of an 'us versus them' approach to entertainment, but that view could also be seen as problematic because no type of gladiator ever, as far as we know, had a name that was evocative of a Roman warrior. Curiously, the plays that the Romans most enjoyed watching as the third century turned into the second were comedies that explicitly took Greek comedies as their models. There were plays on Roman themes including serious dramas – tragedies – that showed scenes from early Roman history or plays set in Rome that were supposedly funny, but they do not seem to have been anything like as popular as the plays in Greek dress. The Greek setting made it possible for sons, slaves and women to make fools out of old men and thus invert the usual authority structure of a Roman household. The audience of comedy watched Roman values being played out and questioned in foreign dress, just as the gladiators' audience watched contests that had taken on aspects of 'foreignness'. The values – courage, strength, speed and skill – were all very Roman, but no Roman was going to lose to a Samnite while they were on display. Is it accidental that the two forms of entertainment should take hold within roughly the same fifty-year period? I doubt it.

Gladiatorial games had become so thoroughly assimilated to the image of Rome by the end of the third century that Antiochus IV included them in the display that he put on to celebrate his own royal power. In Italy, as the first century BC progressed, gladiatorial exhibitions became deeply implicated in the Roman electoral system. Candidates for political office appear to have felt that a really impressive display of gladiators just before an election would enhance their chances of success, so that we find the young Julius Caesar staging games in honour of various family members long after their deaths. It is unlikely that he was the only person to do this, though he seems to have taken things further than others, leading to the first attested decree of the Senate limiting the number of fighting pairs that a politician could put on. Efforts to stem electoral corruption included limitations on a candidate's ability to offer games in the immediate run-up to an election in which he was standing for office. But none of this seems to have worked, and other politicians would employ individual gladiators, and even troupes of them, as bodyguards. Caesar's own collection of gladiators was so immense that special efforts were made to disperse them when the civil war broke out in 49 BC, so that they would not be a threat to public order.[6]

Caesar's gladiators were plainly thought to be loyal to him, suggesting that they were well treated. Indeed, he is said to have had agents throughout Italy who would intervene if it looked as if a promising gladiator was going to be killed, and purchase him for Caesar.[7] This point is of special interest because it suggests that Caesar tried to make sure that his gladiators stayed in one piece.

The notion that the Romans were devoted to watching the slaughter of gladiators in the arena is deeply embedded in the consciousness of Western civilization. Starting in the nineteenth century, if not before – Edward Gibbon, the great historian of the decline and fall of the Roman Empire, was plainly no fan, even if he hardly mentions them – the notion that Romans flocked into amphitheatres to watch gladiators annihilate each other became a powerful symbol of the corruption of Roman imperial society. Gladiatorial combat was a sign that the rot had set in and that the empire must fail. The work of the French painter Jean-Léon Gérôme (1824–1904), whose works include the famous painting of a gladiator standing above his fallen foe and looking up at the bloodthirsty crowd in the amphitheatre, helped inspire Ridley Scott's blockbuster movie *Gladiator*, which has done much to popularize this perception.

It is, however, a view that is fundamentally flawed. First, of course, because gladiatorial combat did not come into being in the era of the emperors, but rather in the era of Rome's greatest expansion. And it had virtually disappeared in the century before the fall of the western empire (traditionally dated to 476 AD), but was still common well into the fourth century when the emperors and most of their subjects were Christians. In other words, there was nothing self-evidently 'pagan' or 'degenerate' about the society in which gladiatorial combat came into being.[8] It may have been cruel – that is entirely another matter – but the people who went to see the games in which gladiators fought did not do so in the expectation of seeing some sort of mass slaughter. If Caesar, the most successful politician in the history of Rome, thought he could get away with saving rather than killing them, and if the next most successful politician in Roman history, Augustus, could, as we shall see, commit himself to making the games less violent, this suggests a strong Roman presumption that death was not a necessary feature of the games.

But although death might not be inevitable, there is no question that people died because they fought as gladiators, and that others could arrange fights where gladiators were killed presumably because they thought that it would make them more popular. In the Roman Republic the killing of a defeated gladiator who had displeased the spectators does not seem to have become especially common – even if Caesar's men were not present to buy a person who was in danger of death – and at that point the individual putting on the games stood to take a financial hit if this happened. A more likely cause of death was simply that the man against whom the gladiator was matched was a menace. This is certainly the situation envisioned in a poem composed by the satirist Lucilius in the late second century BC. In this unique poem, he pictures a fight from the perspective of a gladiator who dreams of skewering his foe. The poem, which we know from quotations in the works of two other authors, seems to have begun with lines introducing the fighters that bring us directly on to the floor of the arena: 'In the games put on by the Flacci, there was a Samnite named Aeserninus, a creep, whose life was worthy of his station. He was matched with Placidianus, who was by far the best of gladiators since the creation of man.' In these lines we hear the voice of the fan, and in the next few those of the gladiator, as Placidianus says to himself:

'I will just kill him and win, if that is what you want,' he said. 'But this is the way that I think it will happen; I will take his blows head on before I stick my sword in the gut and lungs of that jerk. I hate the man. I fight angry, and neither of us will take any longer than it takes while he holds a sword in his right hand, thus am I led by anger, passion and hatred of that man.' (Lucilius 172–81)

The fight seems to have ended with a sword sticking out of someone's stomach. The crucial point here is that Placidianus does not have to kill Aeserninus – he *wants* to kill him, and people will be happy if he does – and the author of these lines sees him as a good man for wanting to do so. Placidianus is choosing the way he will fight and he does so with some notion of the style of his opponent. These are themes that we will encounter in the mouths of gladiators of a later age as well, themes very different from those of the makers of modern films like *Spartacus* or *Gladiator* – although in his version of gladiatorial combat Ridley Scott rightly sees, from the skill and courage he displayed in the amphitheatre, that a man like Maximus could become a hero.[9]

In both *Gladiator* and *Spartacus* (to mention only the best of the lot) gladiators are shown as living in barracks that are no more than prisons. The logic is, of course, that if they were not imprisoned they would simply run away. But very many gladiators were not incarcerated. Julius Caesar's, for instance, were only locked up when they were taken out of their training ground by Caesar's opponents, who feared that they were all too free to come and go as they pleased. Other gladiators could be found living in the houses of the rich and famous, who employed them as bodyguards, as mentioned earlier. Indeed, one of the great domestic crises of the fifties BC occurred when a gladiator who was acting as a bodyguard for a politician murdered that man's rival, Clodius, when the